"Well documented and theoretically sophisticated, this book is a must for all those interested in the independence claims raised in Catalonia and Scotland over the last decade. The authors analyse both cases with a comparative lens while contextualizing the regional secession processes within the framework of European integration. Does the EU facilitate or impede regional secession in the member states? The book's answer is multifaceted as it raises sensitive debates on democracy and self-determination, understood as contestation and politicization vis-à-vis the respective state (Spain and UK)"

Esther Barbé, Universitat Autònoma de Barcelona/
Institut Barcelona d'Estudis Internacionals

"This is an acute analysis of the dilemmas facing Catalan and Scottish nationalists in reconciling nation, state and Europe. It is carefully researched and up to date."

Michael Keating, Emeritus Professor of Politics,
University of Aberdeen

Catalonia, Scotland and the EU

The electoral success of secessionist parties in Catalonia and Scotland over the last decade, together with Brexit and the support for Eurosceptic parties in many European Union (EU) member states, have prompted a rethink of many taken-for-granted notions about politics in Spain, the UK and the EU. Secessionist parties in Catalonia and Scotland often combine calls for independence with support for the EU, but independence for Catalonia might entail the loss of EU membership. In the UK, Scotland voted for the UK to remain in the EU, yet it was forced to leave the Union along with the rest of the country: what effect has Brexit had on Scottish independence claims? Through comparing Catalonia and Scotland, this short volume aims to contribute to debates on, and advance knowledge of, visions of independence and integration, how they interrelate in Europe's emergent political order and what they entail for European integration and democracy in the EU.

Niklas Bremberg is Associate Professor in Political Science at Stockholm University and Senior Research Fellow at the Swedish Institute of International Affairs.

Richard Gillespie is Emeritus Professor of Politics at the University of Liverpool.

Europa Regional Perspectives

Providing in-depth analysis with a global reach, this series from Europa examines a wide range of contemporary political, economic, developmental and social issues in regional perspective. Intended to complement the Europa Regional Surveys of the World series, Europa Regional Perspectives will be a valuable resource for academics, students, researchers, policymakers, business people and anyone with an interest in current world affairs with an emphasis on regional issues.

While the Europa World Year Book and its associated Regional Surveys inform on and analyse contemporary economic, political and social developments, the Editors considered the need for more in-depth volumes written and/or edited by specialists in their field, in order to delve into particular regional situations. Volumes in the series are not constrained by any particular template, but may explore recent political, economic, international relations, social, defence, or other issues in order to increase knowledge. Regions are thus not specifically defined, and volumes may focus on small or large groups of countries, regions or blocs.

The Future of the United States-Australia Alliance
Edited by Scott D. McDonald and Andrew T. H. Tan

External Powers in Latin America
Geopolitics Between Neo-extractivism and South-South Cooperation
Edited by Gian Luca Gardini

The Blue Economy in Sub-Saharan Africa
Working for a Sustainable Future
Edited by Donald L. Sparks

Social Welfare Issues in Southern Europe
Edited by Maria Brown and Michael Briguglio

Catalonia, Scotland and the EU
Visions of Independence and Integration
Niklas Bremberg and Richard Gillespie

For more information about this series, please visit: www.routledge.com/Europa-Regional-Perspectives/book-series/ERP.

Catalonia, Scotland and the EU

Visions of Independence and Integration

Niklas Bremberg and Richard Gillespie

LONDON AND NEW YORK

First published 2022
by Routledge
4 Park Square, Milton Park, Abingdon, Oxon OX14 4RN

and by Routledge
52 Vanderbilt Avenue, New York, NY 10017

Routledge is an imprint of the Taylor & Francis Group, an informa business

© 2022 Niklas Bremberg and Richard Gillespie

The right of Niklas Bremberg and Richard Gillespie to be identified as authors of this work has been asserted in accordance with sections 77 and 78 of the Copyright, Designs and Patents Act 1988.

All rights reserved. No part of this book may be reprinted or reproduced or utilised in any form or by any electronic, mechanical, or other means, now known or hereafter invented, including photocopying and recording, or in any information storage or retrieval system, without permission in writing from the publishers.

Trademark notice: Product or corporate names may be trademarks or registered trademarks, and are used only for identification and explanation without intent to infringe.

British Library Cataloguing in Publication Data
A catalogue record for this book is available from the British Library

Library of Congress Cataloging-in-Publication Data
A catalog record has been requested for this book

ISBN: 978-0-367-65343-9 (hbk)
ISBN: 978-1-032-21135-0 (pbk)
ISBN: 978-1-003-12902-8 (ebk)

DOI: 10.4324/9781003129028

Typeset in Times New Roman
by Taylor & Francis Books

Contents

List of figures		viii
Preface		ix
Abbreviations		xi
1	Studying visions of Scottish and Catalan independence in Europe	1
2	Different paths to independence in Europe	27
3	Catalan independence and European integration: From idealism to realism?	51
4	Scottish independence in an integrated Europe: Still seen as viable?	78
5	Scotland and Catalonia: Comparison and wider implications	102
Appendix		122
Index		124

Figures

1.1 Pro-Scottish independence supporters with Scottish Saltire and EU flags among others including the *estelada*, the unofficial flag of Catalan separatism, at a rally in George Square in Glasgow, Scotland, on 30 July 2016 to call for Scottish independence from the UK   3

1.2 Support for independence in Scotland and Catalonia, 2010–2020   4

3.1 Territorial preferences in the Catalan Parliament, 2010–2021   54

3.2 Trust in the EU by territorial preference in Catalonia, 2013–2017   69

4.1 Scottish elections, 2007–2021   79

4.2 Public attitudes towards the EU in Scotland, 2013–2021   97

Preface

This book is the result of a truly collaborative effort. The idea to write it arose out of our shared and longstanding interest in European, and especially Spanish, politics. Developments in Catalonia and Scotland over the last decade associated with the rise of secessionist politics, including Brexit, have prompted us to rethink and revisit many taken-for-granted notions about politics in Spain, the UK and the European Union (EU). We hope that this book will contribute to debates on, and advance knowledge of, visions of independence and integration, how they interrelate in Europe's emergent political order and what they entail for European integration and democracy in the EU.

The writing of the book has been made possible by a generous research grant from the Marianne and Marcus Wallenberg Foundation (MMW 2017.0027: 'National independence and European integration: Scotland's and Catalonia's democratic challenges to the political order in the EU') and it also draws upon an earlier Economic and Social Research Council project (ES/J007854/1: 'The Dynamics of Nationalist Evolution in Contemporary Spain').

Ideas and draft versions of chapters have been presented at seminars and conferences hosted or organized by the European Consortium for Political Research, the International Studies Association, the Institut Barcelona d'Estudis Internacionals, Lund University, Stockholm University, the Swedish Institute of International Affairs, Stockholm, Queen's University, Kingston, the Université de Montréal-McGill, Montreal, and the Åland Islands Peace Institute, Mariehamn.

Several people have provided us with inspiration, advice, contacts and comments on earlier drafts. We would especially like to mention Rebecca Adler-Nissen, Esther Barbé, Montse Barnadas, Annika Bergman Rosamond, Emil Edenborg, Björn Fägersten, Francesca Guardiola Sala, David G. Haglund, Adam Holesch, Stephen J. Larin, Jane Jenson, Elisabeth Johansson-Nogués, Lena Karlsson, Michael

x *Preface*

Keating, Robert Kissack, Brigid Laffan, Stéphanie Martel, Nicola McEwan, Frédéric Mérand, Margaret Moore, Jasmijn van der Most, Ludvig Norman, William E. Paterson, Mark Rhinard, Ben Rosamond, M. Carme Sans, Andrew Scott, Jonas Tallberg, Martijn Vlaskamp and Marlene Wind.

Finally, we would like to thank our interviewees in Catalonia and Scotland who took the time to answer our questions and provided us with insights into the political dynamics surrounding the discourses and practices through which independence claims are promoted and visions of national independence and European integration are articulated. Details are provided in the Appendix.

Niklas Bremberg and Richard Gillespie
Bromma and Chester, August 2021

Abbreviations

ANC	Assemblea Nacional Catalana (Catalan National Assembly)
CSQP	Catalunya Sí que es Pot (Catalonia Yes We Can)
CDC	Convergència Democràtica de Catalunya (Democratic Convergence of Catalonia)
CEO	Centre d'Estudis d'Opinió
CiU	Convergència i Unió (Convergence and Unity)
CJEU	Court of Justice of the European Union
CoR	Committee of the Regions
Cs	Ciudadanos (Citizens)
CUP	Candidatura d'Unitat Popular (Popular Unity Candidature)
Diplocat	Consell de Diplomàcia Pública de Catalunya (Public Diplomacy Council of Catalonia)
EC	European Community
ECP	En Comú Podem (alliance of Catalunya en Comú and Podem)
EEC	European Economic Community
EFA	European Free Alliance
EP	European Parliament
ERC	Esquerra Republicana de Catalunya (Republican Left of Catalonia)
ETA	Euskadi ta Azkatasuna (Basque Homeland and Liberty)
EU	European Union
ICV	Iniciativa per Catalunya Verds (Initiative for Catalonia Greens)
JxCat	Junts per Catalunya (Together for Catalonia)
JxSí	Junts pel Sí (Together for the Yes)
MEP	Member of the European Parliament

xii *Abbreviations*

MP	Member of Parliament
MSP	Member of the Scottish Parliament
PDeCAT	Partit Demòcrata Europeu Català (Catalan European Democratic Party)
PP	Partido Popular (People's Party)
PSC	Partit dels Socialistes de Catalunya (Socialist Party of Catalonia)
PSOE	Partido Socialista Obrero Español (Spanish Socialist Workers' Party)
SI	Solidaritat Catalana per la Independència (Catalan Solidarity for Independence)
SNP	Scottish National Party
TEU	Treaty on European Union
TFEU	Treaty on the Functioning of the European Union
UDC	Unió Democràtica de Catalunya (Democratic Union of Catalonia)
UN	United Nations
UK	United Kingdom
UP	Unidas Podemos (Together We Can)
USA	United States of America

1 Studying visions of Scottish and Catalan independence in Europe

The European Union (EU) and its member states have in recent decades experienced increasing politicization and contestation around issues of sovereignty and democracy in relation to European supranational competences and decision-making (Abts et al. 2009; Kriesi 2014; Hobolt and Tilley 2016; De Vries 2018). Ever since French and Dutch voters rejected the proposal to establish a Constitution for Europe in 2005, claims to defend national independence against 'Brussels' have definitely moved EU politics from a state of 'permissive consensus' to one of 'constraining dissensus' (Hooghe and Marks 2009). The Brexit referendum in 2016 and the UK's subsequent withdrawal from the EU is perhaps one of the most striking examples of this trend. Furthermore, Eurosceptic parties, often with a populist and right-wing inclination, have gained electoral support in various EU member states, such as Austria, Denmark, France, Germany, Italy, the Netherlands, Spain and Sweden (Akkerman et al. 2016). Typically, these parties depict the EU as deeply undemocratic since bureaucrats rather than elected politicians are said to control the policymaking process in the EU and to marginalize the interests of 'ordinary people' in favour of 'the elite' in Brussels (Müller 2016; Norman 2017). In the discourse of such parties, it is often claimed that the only way for EU member states to restore sovereignty and democracy is to drastically reduce the scope of EU competences and powers, if not to leave the EU entirely (Rydgren 2017).

But there are indications that popular support for EU membership and European integration is still relatively high in many EU member states, and indeed that it has increased in recent years (Eurobarometer 2021: 9). Brexit might even have led to increased support for EU membership in the remaining member states as citizens are 'benchmarking' what leaving the EU would entail in practice (De Vries 2017). The enduring popular appeal of European integration could

DOI: 10.4324/9781003129028-1

2 *Visions of Scottish and Catalan independence in Europe*

also be seen outside the EU in countries such as Ukraine during the Euromaidan crisis of 2014 when protesters in Kiev waved the EU flag in a sign of support for Ukraine's association with the Union. Moreover, political claims are being voiced that seek to advance national independence and challenge the status quo in the EU but not necessarily its competences and powers as such. These claims are often formulated by political parties and movements promoting independence for stateless nations and non-sovereign regions in EU member states, such as Catalonia and Scotland. Even though some secessionist movements in EU member states are decidedly Eurosceptic (such as the Flemish nationalists in Vlaams Belang), in Scotland it is not uncommon to see the EU flag being waved alongside the Scottish Saltire at public manifestations in support of Scottish independence. Similar scenes are often seen in Catalonia, where the EU flag can be spotted alongside the official flag of the Catalan region of Spain (*senyera*) as well as the unofficial Catalan independence flag (*estelada*). Slogans such as that of the Scottish National Party (SNP) 'an independent Scotland in an integrated Europe' or the theme of the pro-independence manifestation in Barcelona in 2012 '*Catalunya, nou estat d'Europa*' ('Catalonia, a new European state') suggest that these political parties and movements often combine their independence claims with explicit support for European integration. This might seem paradoxical to outside observers as it does not necessarily appear self-evident why one should seek national independence for Scotland and Catalonia if one is prepared to have the sovereignty of one's country circumscribed by the supranational competences and powers of the EU.

How can one explain the recent rise in popular support for the independence of stateless nations and non-sovereign regions in EU member states? Why do pro-independence supporters in Catalonia seek independence from Spain when the EU is said to offer enhanced political influence and economic benefits and when Catalan independence might even entail the loss of EU membership? What effects has Brexit had on Scottish independence claims, considering that a majority in Scotland voted for the UK to remain in the EU? By exploring these questions this book addresses central, yet often overlooked, problems in the study of European integration. Focusing on how visions of national independence are articulated in discourse and practice in relation to notions of 'Europe' and European integration in a comparative case study of pro-independence parties in Catalonia and Scotland, this book offers an original contribution to the literature in EU studies and related fields of study on secessionism, independence and integration in Europe.

Visions of Scottish and Catalan independence in Europe 3

Figure 1.1 Pro-Scottish independence supporters with Scottish Saltire and EU flags among others including the *estelada*, the unofficial flag of Catalan separatism, at a rally in George Square in Glasgow, Scotland, on 30 July 2016 to call for Scottish independence from the UK
Source: Andy Buchanan/AFP via Getty Images.

The argument

This book focuses on the type of secessionism that involves sovereignty claims articulated by political actors representing or acting on behalf of stateless nations and non-sovereign regions, primarily in the EU. Regional secessionism in the EU is defined here to include any political project that seeks to turn part of an existing EU member state into an independent state. Despite comparatively high levels of regional autonomy, since 2010 independence claims seem to have resonated with an increasing number of citizens in Catalonia and Scotland (see Figure 1.2).

This book studies and compares the cases of Catalonia and Scotland on the basis that the political dynamics surrounding regional secessionism and European integration in these two cases have been highly salient in recent times (Liñeira and Cetrà 2015; Cuadras-Morató 2016; Closa 2017; Dalle Mulle and Serrano 2019). Advancing our understanding of similarities and differences between Catalan and Scottish independence claims by way of comparing the two cases in a

4 *Visions of Scottish and Catalan independence in Europe*

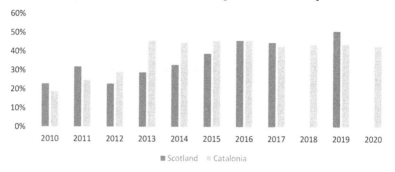

Figure 1.2 Support for independence in Scotland and Catalonia, 2010–2020
Note: Data for Scotland 2018 and 2020 are unavailable.
Source: Centre d'Estudis d'Opinió (2020) and ScotCen Social Research (2020).

European context is important since not all political projects demanding greater regional autonomy in EU member states entail secessionist claims. Some might seek greater devolution in a unitary state or articulate demands for shared sovereignty through a federal or confederal state. Some political parties and movements in EU member states have evolved over time from regionalist and non-independence to secessionist and pro-independence positions (and vice versa). It is therefore of theoretical and methodological importance to try to grasp the political dynamics surrounding national independence and European integration.

Previous research has generated competing theoretical expectations regarding the relationship between regional secessionism, national independence and European integration (Bremberg 2020). One well-established position in the literature is that European integration reduces the mobilizing appeal of independence for regions in the EU due to the effects of economic integration and enhanced possibilities for regions to exercise political influence (Elias 2008; Hepburn 2011). A contrasting position is that European integration does in fact increase the attractiveness of independence because the combined effects of the common market and shared sovereignty make small European states appear more 'viable' in the eyes of regional elites and citizens (Jolly 2007, 2015; Laible 2008). These theoretical accounts seem to be able to explain part of the dynamics in cases such as Catalonia and Scotland, but they do not necessarily help us to understand why, how and under what conditions visions of independence and integration have been articulated in the two cases in recent times and to what extent the dynamics differ between them. Instead,

Visions of Scottish and Catalan independence in Europe 5

the analytical framework developed in this book is based partly on the post-functionalist theory of European integration, which explains the increasing politicization and contestation towards the EU as a function of national identities and elite strategies (Hooghe and Marks 2009). We argue that the focus on the dynamics surrounding national identities is a necessary correction to rationalist and class-based explanations that stipulate that popular support for European integration can be explained mainly in terms of perceived economic gains and political influence, but we also argue that post-functionalism fails to account for how collective identities more generally, and especially within EU member states, are politicized and contested over time. Recent work on secessionism in the EU often fails in this regard too (Duerr 2015). The framework developed in this book therefore seeks to combine post-functionalist insights with a constructivist understanding of political communities (Keating et al. 2019) as well as recent work on the politics of everyday Europe and the symbols and practices through which the EU becomes a social fact in the lived experience of EU citizens (Manners 2011; Adler-Nissen 2016; McNamara 2016).

We argue that in order to grasp the mobilizing potential of independence claims in Scotland and Catalonia, close attention needs to be paid to why and how pro-independence parties and movements frame their claims as congruent with visions of an integrated Europe. Contrary to what scholars might have expected a few decades ago, European integration has not led to national identities losing their political significance. What seems to be particularly interesting in the two cases is that the increase in popular support for independence suggests a convergence of nationalist activism with non-nationalist segments of Catalan and Scottish societies that perceive independence more as a democratizing objective. It thus needs to be better explained and understood how and with what effects claims to defend 'European values' and to forge 'an ever closer union of the peoples of Europe' can, in practice, be made to resonate with claims for Catalan and Scottish independence.

Regional secessionism and European integration in historical perspective

In the classic works on state-building in Europe, sovereignty (de jure and de facto control over a delimited, geographical territory by a state) and secession (the act by which part of a sovereign state

6 *Visions of Scottish and Catalan independence in Europe*

establishes itself as a new state) are often treated as two sides of the same coin (Rokkan and Urwin 1983; Tilly 1992). Since the end of the devastating Second World War and as a result of the creation of the United Nations, the principles of state sovereignty and national self-determination have been considered to be cornerstones of international law, although they are not always easy to reconcile in practice. In Europe, many states can be said to have various economic and political centres, multiple national identities and several official languages. Several European states, and not only the federal ones, have established constitutional arrangements that seek to recognize such social and political realities by guaranteeing rights for ethnic and linguistic minorities and advancing regional autonomy, for example. Managing the political, economic and social tensions between centre and periphery arising from competing demands on resources and representation is a fundamental aspect of many democratic states in Europe and the trend towards increased decentralization in several European states is often referred to as a response to such enduring tensions (Keating 1998). There is nonetheless a difference between decentralization in states where state boundaries are not challenged (such as the Netherlands, Portugal and Sweden), and in states where competing visions of nationhood exist (such as Belgium, Spain and the UK). In the second case, decentralization has often been described as a means to neutralize independence claims by way of offering greater regional autonomy (Moreno 2001).

Another important difference is that between unitary and federal states, as the latter usually recognize that state sovereignty is shared among the component states. In the context of this book it is worth mentioning that both Spain and the UK can be described as unitary states with comparatively advanced levels of regional autonomy. Catalan regional autonomy within the Spanish state was re-established under the Generalitat de Catalunya (Government of Catalonia) as part of the democratization of Spain in the 1970s (Colino 2020). The statute that regulates Catalan autonomy was initially introduced after a popular referendum in October 1979 (supported by 90 per cent of voters on a turnout of 59 per cent). Catalonia currently has a high degree of autonomy on issues related to education, health care and policing. Following a referendum in Scotland in 1997 (supported by 74 per cent of voters on a turnout of 60 per cent), the UK Parliament passed the Scotland Act in 1998 through which various 'devolved competencies' were transferred to the Scottish Parliament (McTavish and Garnett 2020). These competencies were later expanded in 2012 and 2016 and currently cover education, health care, agriculture and

Visions of Scottish and Catalan independence in Europe 7

the judiciary. It is also worth mentioning that the UK was originally created as a union of two kingdoms as a result of the Treaty of Union 1707, whereas according to the current Spanish Constitution of 1978, Spain's sovereignty is indissoluble (Elliot 2018). This is often suggested to provide the different legal reasons as to why the UK Government could agree to the Scottish independence referendum in 2014, and why the Spanish state cannot accept a Catalan referendum on independence (Cetrà and Liñera 2018).

Since the demise of the Soviet Union and the break-up of Yugoslavia, secessionist movements have gained increased attention as political phenomena among social scientists, not least in the fields of Political Science and International Relations (Buchanan 2007; Roeder 2007). However, the evidence from 1945 onwards suggests that secession is a rather rare phenomenon among well-functioning democracies in Europe (Sorens 2012). Political parties and movements that peacefully propagate in favour of independence and secession are nonetheless tolerated in basically all democratic states in Europe, but the right to secede is typically not granted in national constitutions. For instance, the German Constitutional Court's ruling in 2016 stipulated that a referendum on Bavarian independence cannot be held since the Constitution of the Federal Republic of Germany does not allow it (Bundesverfassungsgericht 2016). In other words, in most European states, campaigning for regional secession is allowed but such claims cannot be put into practice, at least not unless proper constitutional changes are made (Reinikainen 2019). This is of course related to the respect for the rule of law in liberal democracies and to the deeply ingrained norm that the state borders that emerged in Europe after the Second World War should not be violated, unless it is done peacefully and as a result of negotiations (Kornprobst 2008). In relation to this question, the Canadian Clarity Act of 1998 is often referred to as an example of how democratic states can address secessionist claims in a constructive fashion. The act made clear that no Canadian province has the right to secede from Canada by unilaterally declaring independence, but if a clear majority of the population in a province express support for independence, then the Federal Government of Canada should seek a negotiated solution (Dion 2012).

In the context of this book it is important to note that regional secessionism in the EU has taken on a rather different meaning compared to other parts of the world (Keating 2019; Bauböck 2019). This is related to the European integration process which has reshaped relations between the supranational, national and regional levels of governance in EU member states (Bartolini 2005; Jordana et al. 2019).

8 *Visions of Scottish and Catalan independence in Europe*

Some scholars describe the EU as a 'post-sovereign' political system, whereas others stress the less dramatic but still profound shift from European *nation* states to *member* states of the EU (Keating 2001; Bickerton 2012). European integration has also been understood as a process that has reduced territorial tensions between centre and periphery within many EU member states and has fostered peaceful cooperation among them (Linz and Stepan 1996; Bremberg 2018). Others suggest that member state sovereignty in the EU has been undermined as an increasing number of 'core state functions' have gradually been integrated into the EU's political system (Genschel and Jachtenfuchs 2016; Mair 2013). Still others point to the fact that despite decades of integration EU member states have been able to reassert their influence on decision-making in the EU, not least in the context of the growing importance of the European Council (van Middelaar 2013).

The developments in Europe from the 1990s onwards as a result of the ratification of the Treaty on European Union (TEU) have meant that the political status of regions in EU member states has changed. It should be said that the concept of 'region' in the EU refers to a quite heterogenous set of sub-state entities. For example, the EU's Committee of the Regions (CoR) is composed of 350 members representing local (including municipalities and cities) and regional (including autonomous regions as well as administrative units) levels. The CoR can make recommendations and proposals on EU laws and policies, but it is ultimately the member states that appoint CoR members, and the European Commission and the Council of the EU mainly consult the Committee on matters of social and territorial cohesion, regional development, and employment.

However, regional secessionism in the EU increasingly provokes questions on citizenship and democracy in Europe. Debates on democracy in the EU tend to repeat the trope that the EU is characterized by a 'democratic deficit' as EU decision-making procedures are not held accountable to the same extent as those in national political systems (Bellamy and Castiglione 2000; Føllesdal and Hix 2006). However, some question whether the EU has a democratic deficit at all, since the political authority of the EU is delegated from its member states (Brexit suggests that it can be revoked), and decision-making rests on the legal principles enshrined in the EU treaties (Majone 1998; Moravscik 2002). In practice, these matters are quite complicated, particularly since EU citizenship was introduced with the ratification of the TEU (Seubert et al. 2018). It stipulates that any person who is a citizen of an EU member state is automatically also

Visions of Scottish and Catalan independence in Europe 9

an EU citizen. EU citizenship grants certain rights that extend beyond national citizenship, such as freedom of movement and residence within the whole Union, to vote and stand as a candidate in elections for the European Parliament and in municipal elections in the country of residence, and the protection of the diplomatic and consular authorities of any EU member state outside of the Union. Even though these rights are ultimately dependent on national citizenship, they suggest that individuals are recognized as being subject to EU law beyond the rights and duties conferred on them by regulations governing the functioning of the EU's internal market (Kenealy 2014).

Competing views on regional secessionism and European integration

The mobilizing appeal that sovereignty claims enjoy in Scotland and Catalonia suggests that questions of how to explain and understand the links between regional secession, national independence and European integration are far from settled. The process of European integration seems to have opened up new avenues for politicization and contestation within EU member states around issues of sovereignty, secessionism and self-determination. This might seem paradoxical, at least if it is assumed that secessionist claims should diminish as an effect of European integration. Several scholars have argued in favour of this view for a number of interrelated reasons. First, changes in the 1980s and 1990s regarding EU structural funding, together with the legal and institutional developments (TEU, CoR), created new opportunities for regional political elites to gain access to resources and to participate in EU policymaking (Elias 2008). Second, the strengthening of region-level political institutions in many Western European states empowered regional elites to develop new strategies for securing funds and access to political arenas beyond their 'host states' (Marks et al. 1996). Third, the electoral successes of many pro-independence political parties at the regional level in several EU member states meant that they often had to transform themselves from single-issue parties to 'normal' parties, situate themselves on the left-right ideological spectrum and respond to multiple policy issues. Taken together, these factors were seen as facilitating a trend in which radical demands for independence were gradually changed into more moderate calls for greater regional autonomy (Hepburn 2011). Over time, these trends were thought likely to diminish the appeal of independence claims in Scotland, Catalonia and other regions across the EU.

10 *Visions of Scottish and Catalan independence in Europe*

However, these theoretically informed expectations do not correspond with more recent developments in Scotland and Catalonia. While a majority of Scottish voters voted against independence in the 2014 referendum (55 per cent voted 'no' on a turnout of 84 per cent), support for Scottish independence has remained at historically high levels at above 40 per cent, and some polls suggest that support for independence is currently over 50 per cent (see above). In 2017, in Catalonia, some 42 per cent of eligible voters participated in an unconstitutional 'referendum' organized by the Catalan regional government, and an overwhelmingly majority of those who participated voted in favour of independence. The Spanish Constitutional Court had previously ruled that the Catalan Government did not have the authority to organize a referendum on independence (not unlike the ruling by the German Constitutional Court in 2016). It should be said that so far there are no overwhelming majorities in favour of independence in either Scotland or Catalonia. Nonetheless, the majority position among the pro-secessionist political parties and movements in both cases is to strive for national independence and membership of the EU at the same time.

The viability theory seeks to explain this seemingly paradoxical situation from a different vantage point (Jolly 2007, 2015; Laible 2008). The theory suggests that the EU should be seen as a factor that actually makes secessionist claims more attractive in the eyes of political elites and citizens in certain regions of the EU. Based on a study of several regionalist and secessionist parties across EU member states, Jolly (2007) has argued that there is evidence that EU membership and European integration are perceived as making small states more 'viable' because the political and economic benefits of belonging to a larger state decrease when the new state can be thought of as being a future member of the EU. Over time, the argument goes, European integration has made it possible for regional elites to more credibly portray regional secessionism as a viable political strategy, since the EU provides a common European market, a single European currency and enhanced European cooperation on foreign and security policy. Cram has noted that 'the EU can play an instrumental role, for example in Catalonia and Scotland, making nationalist demands more palatable in the context of a stabilising framework' (2009: 105). The fact that the UK and Spain provided national markets, currencies and military defence to Scotland and Catalonia in the past does not mean that these host states will always have to do so. Rather, it can arguably be seen as a historical condition that no longer applies in contemporary Europe. In the eyes of pro-independence supporters, it

Visions of Scottish and Catalan independence in Europe 11

might seem perfectly reasonable to argue that if relatively small states such as Ireland and Denmark can thrive as EU member states why should Scotland and Catalonia not be able to do the same?

The European Commission's response to regional secessionism in the EU

Thus, it can be argued that regional secessionism and European integration do not necessarily stand in contradiction to each other but can be mutually reinforcing. But the fact that political leaders and citizens in Scotland and Catalonia embrace this view does not mean that EU membership would automatically follow at independence. Judging from what representatives of the European Commission have said on this matter, it seems that a newly independent European state wishing to become an EU member state needs to apply for membership and wait in line with the rest of the candidate countries, regardless of the fact that it might previously have been part of another EU member state. In addition, the Commission's official position is that Catalan and Scottish independence are to be regarded as 'internal matters' of sovereign member states and thus not things that it should be involved in. In 2004, the former President of the Commission, Romano Prodi, outlined a sort of doctrine with regard to regional secessionism in the EU:

> When a part of a territory of a Member State ceases to be part of that state, i.e. because that territory becomes an independent state, the Treaties no longer apply to that territory. In other words, a newly independent region would, by the fact of its independence, become a third country with respect to the Union and the Treaties would, from the day of its independence, not apply anymore on its territory.
>
> (Cited in Piris 2017a: 82)

Both José Manuel Durão Barroso and Jean-Claude Juncker, who succeeded Prodi at the helm of the European Commission, stated on numerous occasions that the Prodi doctrine applied. The doctrine basically stipulates that any part of an EU member state that becomes an independent state needs to reapply for EU membership according to Article 49 TEU and then follow the standard membership application procedure.[1] In practice, this means that the Commission would first need to assess whether the new state meets all the requirements for EU membership and the existing EU member states would eventually have to agree unanimously to accept the new state as a member.

12   *Visions of Scottish and Catalan independence in Europe*

Obviously, such a process could take a considerable amount of time. Turkey, although perhaps not a typical case, has been an official EU candidate country since 2005. Furthermore, it is not impossible that some EU member states would object to admitting the new state for various political reasons. For example, Cyprus, Greece, Slovakia, Spain and Romania have not recognized Kosovo as an independent country, which makes it impossible for Kosovo to initiate accession negotiations with the EU.

But the doctrine can be questioned on both legal and normative grounds. First, it is not entirely clear whether the Commission's position is based on international law or EU law (cf. Weiler 1991; MacCormick 1997). The Court of Justice of the EU (CJEU) argues that EU law constitutes a distinct legal order that goes beyond international law and by implication 'standard' legal interpretations of how to deal with state secession. Second, the EU is often portrayed as different from state-centric international organizations, which is seen in relation to the obligations of EU member states to respect EU citizenship rights, for example. The EU treaties (Article 20 TEU and Article 20(1) TFEU) make it clear that EU citizenship is supplementary to citizenship of member states but 'a series of judicially activist rulings by the [CJEU] has caused a sort of schizophrenia at the heart of the concept of EU citizenship. It exists in the Treaties as one thing, and it exists in the jurisprudence of the [CJEU] as something considerably more far-reaching' (Kenealy 2014: 591). Third, one of the main tasks bestowed on the Commission is to protect the integrity of the EU's internal market. Obviously, forcing a region of a member state to leave the EU would create a sharp dislocation within the market and deprive millions of persons of their rights as EU citizens.

Interestingly, the Commission appears to have arrived at an interpretation of the EU treaties that seems to be based on an exclusion mechanism that does not exist. The withdrawal mechanism that does exist in the treaties is Article 50 TEU, which was invoked by the UK Government in March 2017 in order to commence the Brexit negotiations. This article assumes that it is impossible to throw out an EU member state overnight, since the integration of economic activities, harmonization of rules and regulations, and deepening of cooperation in various policy fields has reached such an advanced stage. Instead, it stipulates that withdrawal needs to be accomplished through a negotiated transition, and that the negotiations need to take account of the future relationship between the EU and the withdrawing state.

While it is perhaps not hard to understand the political reasoning that underpins the Prodi doctrine and the reasons for which the

Visions of Scottish and Catalan independence in Europe 13

Commission has decided to side with EU member states in matters related to regional secessionism in the EU, it can be argued that doing so might risk increasing the tensions between the notions of 'Europe of the states' and 'Europe of the citizens' in ways that neither strengthen support for European integration nor lead to a decrease in popular support for independence in Catalonia or Scotland. There are also reasons to believe that the CJEU would not automatically support the Commission's position if a region of an EU member state became an independent state, albeit that the Court would most likely pay close attention to how the secession process unfolded in practice (unconstitutional and unilateral acts of secession would probably not be recognized) (Kenealy 2014).

Moreover, it has been suggested that if a region or another territory were to secede from an EU member state it should be understood as an instance of 'territorial rescaling' and 'a move to change the status or affiliation of a territory within a wider constellation of polities' (Bauböck 2019: 3). Bauböck has noted that the ways in which the legal and normative challenges spurred by the Prodi doctrine are interpreted depend to a large extent on whether the EU is understood as a federation in the making or a voluntary association of independent states. Prior to the UK's departure from the EU he argued that Catalan or Scottish independence would undoubtedly put these territories outside the EU, although 'the fact that EU law had been deeply entrenched in all these polities while they were inside should facilitate negotiations about terms of separation in the former case and of accession in the latter, but it does not affect the question of membership status itself' (Bauböck 2019: 15). Of course, the fact that the doctrine can be criticized for making the Commission less constructive than it might ideally be in handling these complex matters, is not the same as saying that it is an easy task to determine what would happen if a non-sovereign region of the EU were to become an independent state. This uncertainty might be a reason for caution, in the sense that when political leaders and citizens are forced to consider the likelihood of different outcomes of a hypothetical secession process it might be assumed that not knowing what would happen with the relationship with the EU would act as a deterrent. Politics, however, do not always work that way.

In fact, uncertainty might in some cases encourage risk-taking among citizens, especially if political leaders imply that the Commission is bluffing and that one can have national independence and EU membership at the same time. This would imply that what really matters is how credible citizens believe the Prodi doctrine to be and what they think the EU and its member states would actually do if a region

14 *Visions of Scottish and Catalan independence in Europe*

really did become an independent state through secession. Judging from recent developments in Scotland and Catalonia, it appears that a not insignificant number of Scottish and Catalan citizens think that the Commission's position is not entirely credible or at least that they are prepared to take a chance that it is not. It could also be that some are willing to accept a period of disruption to EU membership if that is seen as what it would take to achieve independence. Still others might not actually care very much about EU membership, and it could be that those citizens that most ardently support independence for Scotland and Catalonia are actually the ones who feel the least attachment to the EU (Muro and Vlaskamp 2016).

Post-functionalism, constructivism and the politics of 'everyday Europe'

The study upon which this book rests departs from the notion that political arguments for and against regional secessionism in the EU need to be articulated in relation to and resonate with understandings of the normative and democratic foundations of the EU's political order. To study why, how and under what conditions independence claims for stateless nations and non-sovereign regions are formulated in the EU, we suggest an analytical framework that partly builds upon post-functionalist theory of European integration (Hooghe and Marks 2009). Previous research has suggested that, in general, factors such as socio-economic status and level of education explain public support for European integration, albeit with significant cross-national variances (Favell 2008; Fligstein 2008). Moreover, there is evidence to suggest that people who tend to think of themselves as having a strong European identity also show high levels of support for EU membership and European integration, although the sense of European identity seldom trumps national identities in EU member states (Hooghe and Marks 2004; Checkel and Katzenstein 2009; Harteveld et al. 2013). However, there is also evidence that in certain contexts a sense of belonging to Europe reinforces collective identities other than the national identity of an EU member state. This seems to be the case in Catalonia where many Catalans express a sense of being more European and Catalan than Spanish (Diez Medrano 2010). The Brexit referendum seems to suggest something similar in terms of the different levels of attachment to Europe when Scottish and English voters are compared (Curtice and Montagu 2020).

The post-functionalist theory of European integration explains the increasing politicization and contestation towards the EU as a

Visions of Scottish and Catalan independence in Europe 15

function of exclusive national identities and elite strategies. Hooghe and Marks suggest that European integration as a process is largely spurred by the need of European states to effectively manage various political and economic pressures stemming from globalization forces, market actors and citizens' demands.[2] However, the outcome of the process does not necessarily 'reflect functional pressures, or even that the outcome will reflect these pressures mediated by their distributional consequences' (Hooghe and Marks 2009: 2). Instead, political conflict is assumed to determine the course of European integration to a much higher extent. Hooghe and Marks argue that currently there is a tension between jurisdictional developments at the EU level and the endurance of national identities in member states. However, such tension is not an unavoidable effect of European integration as such. Instead 'political entrepreneurs must mobilize the tension' (ibid.: 13). This is because for most people the relationship between national identity and European integration cannot be evoked directly from personal experience. The link needs to be constructed, and in practice this is often done in relation to salient events such as EU enlargement, treaty reforms, austerity measures, migration crises, Brexit, etc. Hooghe and Marks also suggest that it is common for individuals to feel a strong sense of national belonging yet remain positively oriented towards European integration. Negative attitudes towards European integration and EU membership are rather a result of people perceiving their national identity as being predominantly exclusive (ibid.).

In our view, focusing on identity dynamics and political mobilizing is a necessary correction to rationalist or class-based explanations that stipulate support for European integration in terms of economic gains and, possibly, political influence. But we argue that the dynamics of collective identities in many European states are not only determined by the binary logic of being 'exclusive' and 'inclusive' in relation to the sense of national belonging versus a sense of affiliation with Europe. This is because there might exist various national identities within an EU member state, which is the case in countries such as Spain and the UK. Thus, it is reasonable to assume that the meaning of European integration and EU membership might vary within and among member states as a result of how dominant national identities are constructed in relation to other communities that perceive themselves as nations without a state of their own. In contrast to post-functionalism, our framework rests explicitly on a constructivist understanding of political communities which ultimately sees self-determination as a claim that rests on an ontological component (i.e. a group existing as a social and political reality) and a normative component (i.e. the

16 *Visions of Scottish and Catalan independence in Europe*

notion that the group has a right to meaningfully govern itself in relation to others) (Keating et al. 2019: 11). In this way we argue that our framework is better equipped to analyse the particular dynamics involving national identities in the context of regional secessionism in the EU.

Our framework combines constructivist and post-functionalist insights with recent work on the politics of everyday Europe as this strand of research focuses on the symbols and practices through which the EU becomes a social fact in the lived experience of EU citizens (Manners 2011; Adler-Nissen 2016; McNamara 2016). McNamara argues that:

> By changing the lived experience of what Europe is, the symbols and practices at work in Europe today make natural a deepening of political power at the European level, while constructing 'Europeans.' These cultural processes work to create the EU as a social fact, that is, a widely shared intersubjective understanding that seems to exist on its own, separate from us, even as it relies on our collective agreement for its existence.
>
> (2016: 3)

In our view, the important insight here is that people might feel closely attached to 'Europe' due to their life experiences, professional careers and education, but this does not have to imply that EU membership is seen as something uncontroversial. Rather, it might be that a sense of being 'European' is combined with certain expectations that resonate with political claims in relation to social rights, economic well-being or democratic governance. It might even be connected to a sense of being entitled to national self-determination in a democratic community of European states and peoples. We argue that in order to grasp the mobilizing potential of claims to independence for stateless nations and non-sovereign regions in the EU, close attention needs to be paid to the way in which pro-independence parties and movements articulate and frame their claims as congruent with visions of an integrated Europe. Contrary to what some scholars seem to have expected a few decades ago, European integration has not led to national identities losing their political significance, as claims to defend 'European values' and to forge 'an ever closer union of the peoples of Europe' can be made to resonate with claims for Catalan and Scottish independence in ways that clearly challenge the territorial status quo in Spain and the UK, albeit not necessarily the normative and democratic foundations of the EU.

Visions of Scottish and Catalan independence in Europe 17

To illustrate how the theoretical assumptions that underpin our analytical framework can structure analyses of the Catalan and Scottish cases, we might consider that although Catalan independence would obviously upset the territorial integrity of Spain it does not necessarily challenge the competences and powers of the EU per se. Representatives of the Catalan Government as well as pro-independence parties have argued that since the Spanish Government refuses to negotiate the terms of a legal referendum on independence, Catalonia is left with no other means than to seek to organize one outside of Spanish legality. In October 2017, a 'referendum' on Catalan independence was organized. The Spanish Constitutional Court had previously ruled it to be unconstitutional and Spanish police forces tried to prevent people from taking part, violently at times. Although the results of the 'referendum' were questioned on procedural grounds by many observers, the President of the Catalan Government at the time, Carles Puigdemont, argued that they legitimized the Catalan Parliament to declare independence. However, immediately after the Catalan Parliament had done so, he went into exile in Brussels, Belgium. The Spanish Government temporarily suspended Catalan regional autonomy and several Catalan politicians who were charged with organizing the 2017 'referendum' were later convicted for crimes such as sedition and/or misuse of public funds and sentenced to harsh prison sentences, among them the leader of Esquerra Republicana de Catalunya (ERC), Oriol Junqueras. What is interesting in the context of our framework is that many pro-independence politicians in Catalonia voiced their disappointment with, in their view, the feeble response of the EU in the face of what they saw as Spanish state repression. For example, Puigdemont posted a message on Twitter in November 2017 rhetorically asking 'Is this the Europe you want to build? How long can Europe ignore what is happening in Catalonia?'

The Scottish case has many interesting parallels with Catalonia, albeit several important differences as well, which are relevant in view of our analytical framework. One major difference is that the UK and Scottish Governments managed to agree on the format for a referendum on Scottish independence held in 2014. But since the Brexit referendum in 2016 (in which a majority of Scottish voters voted in favour of remaining in the EU), the Scottish Government has repeatedly argued that Scottish independence is the only way for Scotland to rejoin the EU. That the UK Government did not allow the Scottish Government a seat at the table during the Brexit negotiations was also depicted as causing serious harm to Scotland's interests. The UK Supreme Court ruling on the UK Government's enactment of Article

18   *Visions of Scottish and Catalan independence in Europe*

50 TEU stipulated that the Government needed to secure parliamentary approval. However, the Court also ruled that the UK Government did not have to seek approval from the Scottish Parliament since it is not considered to be a sovereign parliament as its powers are ultimately devolved from Westminster. After the UK withdrew from the EU in January 2020, Nicola Sturgeon, SNP leader and First Minister of Scotland, published a statement asking 'our friends in Europe to leave a light on for Scotland so we can find our way home [since] being part of the EU is an expression of shared values we hold dear, the ideas of solidarity, openness and a genuine partnership of equal nations' (cited in SNP 2020).

The analytical framework developed in this book seeks to enable analysis of how and to what extent independence and secessionist claims articulate visions of European integration, and how and to what extent such claims open up a symbolic struggle over the meaning of values that the EU is supposed to advance or protect, such as freedom, democracy and human rights. It is assumed that representatives of the EU as well as of the UK and Spanish Governments need to counter Scottish and Catalan independence claims in ways that are deemed consistent with what are understood to be basic democratic as well as legal principles in EU and international law, and that this in practice is defining the boundaries of the symbolic struggle. In line with the framework's constructivist assumptions, this struggle is understood as a fundamentally political meaning-making activity which draws on discourses and practices inherent to the process of European integration as it has developed over more than half a century. In essence, taking the notion that 'we belong in Europe' for granted might be something that makes independence claims appear not only attractive in the eyes of many citizens in Catalonia and Scotland: it might even make the notion of national independence in Europe appear self-evident to them, and to oppose this might increase their sense of a wrongdoing being committed.

The reasons underpinning claims for Catalan and Scottish independence need not be exactly the same across the two cases, but our framework enables us to highlight the political and normative contestation that such claims articulate in relation to visions of national independence and European integration. Furthermore, the meaning ascribed to European integration and EU membership might differ over time as well as between the two cases, but the theoretical assumptions underpinning our framework suggest that the mobilizing appeal of national independence and European integration might reinforce each other, even though answering questions about why, how

Visions of Scottish and Catalan independence in Europe 19

and under what conditions they do so needs to be explored empirically.

Research design, case selection and data collection

This book rests on a comparative case study of Scottish and Catalan independence claims in the context of European integration. The empirical analysis is mainly directed towards the period 2010–2021, although earlier periods are also covered to provide a historical context to more recent developments. The Scottish and Catalan cases were selected out of the larger population of possible cases of stateless nations and non-sovereign regions in the EU with secessionist and pro-independence parties and movements mainly on the basis of two criteria: *salience* and *coherence*. Among the relevant cases in the EU, Scotland and Catalonia are currently the two most salient as the issue of independence is high on the political agenda in both countries. Choosing Scotland and Catalonia also implies studying two relatively coherent cases characterized by a strong sense of national identity based on history and culture, as well as advanced levels of regional autonomy. Both cases are also linked by the use of contemporaneous referendums (albeit that the Scottish referendum on independence held in 2014 was legal, whereas the 'referendum' organized in Catalonia in 2017 was unconstitutional). Equally important, the cases *differ* in their economic status within the context of their host states as well as in terms of historical experiences of democratic rule and EU membership (Elliot 2018). Another important difference is that in Scotland there is one dominant pro-independence party, the SNP, whereas in Catalonia there are several pro-independence parties that compete for political dominance, such as ERC, Junts per Catalunya, the Partit Demòcrata Europeu Català, the former Convergència Democràtica de Catalunya, and the Candidatura d'Unitat Popular. In addition, civil society organizations, such as the Assemblea Nacional de Catalunya, have featured more influentially in the Catalan case.

Furthermore, in the post-Brexit setting Scottish independence claims are increasingly being legitimized as a way for Scotland to rejoin the EU, whereas Catalan independence claims must still be justified against the risk of possibly losing EU membership. With the empirical analysis covering the period 2010–2021 it is possible to study to what extent independence claims in Scotland have changed in the post-Brexit setting as well as to explore the shifting political landscape in Catalonia since independence became a major political issue after 2012. Thus, overlaps between the two cases are large enough to make

20 *Visions of Scottish and Catalan independence in Europe*

comparison meaningful and the differences that exist ensure a level of variety that allows for exploring different ways in which independence claims relate to the symbolic struggle over the meaning of European integration and EU membership.

A version of discourse analysis is applied in both cases to study how independence claims are presented, justified and contested in relation to notions of 'Europe', EU membership and European integration. Independence has been high on the political agenda recently, but popular support for independence in Catalonia and Scotland has fluctuated over time and the same applies to Scottish and Catalan attitudes towards the EU, which makes it important to study how independence claims are framed in relation to 'Europe' and to what extent they change, as a means to understand the dynamics inherent to the symbolic struggle around national independence and European integration. Important data sources collected for the comparative case study include official statements from national and regional governments, party leaders and representatives as well as from EU institutions. Other important data sources are party congresses and electoral manifestos from pro-independence parties presented ahead of national, regional and European elections.

In addition, semi-structured interviews with political representatives from Scottish and Catalan pro-independence parties have been conducted to map how these political actors understand and make strategic use of arguments for independence in a European context (see Appendix). These interviews constitute an important source of data on practical dispositions and background knowledge necessary to competently perform independence claims in the Scottish and Catalan contexts, and they might also provide clues as to how 'being European' or 'belonging to Europe' are performed by political actors in these different settings. Furthermore, public opinion data on attitudes towards European integration and EU membership in Scotland and Catalonia as well as research on popular support for Scottish and Catalan independence have been analysed and compared to assess the broader social conditions under which politicization and contestation around independence and integration are performed in the two cases. The combination of analysis of party discourse, elite interviews and public opinion makes this comparative case study uniquely equipped to explore Scottish and Catalan independence claims, and thus contribute to our understanding of the relationship between national identities and elite strategies in the political dynamics surrounding regional secessionism in the EU.

Outline of the book

This book contains five chapters, including this Introduction. Chapter 2 describes how the main secessionist parties in Scotland and Catalonia articulated their visions of independence and integration in a European context up until 2010 in order to highlight the extent to which the political dynamics surrounding the question of national independence and European integration converged and diverged between the two cases. Chapter 3 on Catalonia and Chapter 4 on Scotland provide the basis for comparing developments since 2010 by way of (a) analysing how the pro-independence parties have tried to discursively use 'Europe' in the furtherance of their objectives; (b) evaluating public opinion on the level of support for independence and EU membership; and (c) assessing the assumptions that pro-independence parties have made about European responses to their independence claims and to what extent they have changed their views on the EU in view of its opposition to secessionism. Chapter 5 summarizes and compares the findings from the analyses of the two cases and discusses what this implies for the book's main questions on regional secessionism and European integration.

Notes

1 For an overview of the legal reasoning underpinning the Prodi doctrine, see Piris (2017a, 2017b).
2 This is also assumed in the classic theories of European integration, such as neo-functionalism (Haas 1958) and intergovernmentalism (Moravcsik 1998).

References

Abts, Koen, Heerwegh, Dirk and Swyngedouw, Marc (2009). Sources of Euroscepticism: Utilitarian interest, social distrust, national identity and institutional distrust. *World Political Science Review*, 5 (1): 1–26.
Adler-Nissen, Rebecca (2016). Towards a practice turn in EU studies: The everyday of European integration. *Journal of Common Market Studies*, 54 (1): 87–103.
Akkerman, Tjitske, de Lange, Sarah L. and Rooduijn, Matthijs (eds) (2016). *Radical right-wing populist parties in Western Europe: Into the mainstream?* London: Routledge.
Bartolini, Stefano (2005). *Restructuring Europe: Centre formation, system building, and political structuring between the nation state and the European Union.* Oxford: Oxford University Press.
Bauböck, Rainer (2019). A multilevel theory of democratic secession. *Ethnopolitics*, 18 (3): 227–246.

22 *Visions of Scottish and Catalan independence in Europe*

Bellamy, Richard and Castiglione, Dario (2000). Reflections on the European democratic deficit. In Erik O. Eriksen and Jon E. Fossum (eds), *Democracy in the European Union: Integration through deliberation?* London: Routledge, 65–84.

Bickerton, Christopher (2012). *European integration: From nation-states to member states.* Oxford: Oxford University Press.

Bremberg, Niklas (2018). The EU and the European security community: History and current challenges. In Antonina Bakardjieva Engelbrekt, Anna Michalski, Niklas Nilsson and Lars Oxelheim (eds), *The European Union: Facing the challenge of multiple security threats.* Cheltenham: Edward Elgar Publishing, 18–41.

Bremberg, Niklas (2020). The dream of the nation-state: Is regional secessionism a threat to European integration? In Antonina Bakardjieva Engelbrekt, Anna Michalski, Karin Leijon and Lars Oxelheim (eds), *The European Union and the return of the nation-state.* Cham: Palgrave Macmillan, 241–267.

Buchanan, Allen E. (2007). *Justice, legitimacy, and self-determination: Moral foundations for international law.* Oxford: Oxford University Press.

Bundesverfassungsgericht (2016). *Beschluss der 2. Kammer des Zweiten Senats, 2 BvR 349/16.* 16 December. Available at www.bundesverfassungsgericht.de/Sha redDocs/Entscheidungen/DE/2016/12/rk20161216_2bvr034916.html (accessed 9 June 2021).

Centro d'Estudis d'Opinió (2020). *Encuesta sobre contexto político en Cataluña.* Barcelona: Generalitat de Catalunya.

Cetrà, Daniel and Liñeira, Robert (2018). Breaking-up within Europe: Substate nationalist strategies in multilevel polities. *Journal of Common Market Studies*, 56 (3): 717–729.

Checkel, Jeffrey T. and Katzenstein, Peter J. (eds) (2009). *European identity.* Cambridge: Cambridge University Press.

Closa, Carlos (ed.) (2017). *Secession from a member state and withdrawal from the European Union: Troubled membership.* Cambridge: Cambridge University Press.

Colino, César (2020). Decentralization in Spain: Federal evolution and performance of the estado autonómico. In Diego Muro and Ignacio Lago (eds), *The Oxford handbook of Spanish politics.* Oxford: Oxford University Press.

Cram, Laura (2009). Introduction: Banal Europeanism: European Union identity and national identities in synergy. *Nations and Nationalism*, 15 (1): 101–108.

Cuadras-Morató, Xavier (ed.) (2016). *Catalonia: A new independent state in Europe? A debate on secession within the European Union.* London: Routledge.

Curtice, John and Montagu, Ian (2020). *Is Brexit fuelling support for independence?* What Scotland Thinks. Available at https://whatscotlandthinks. org/wp-content/uploads/2020/11/SSA-2019-Scotland-paper-v5.pdf (accessed 21 May 2021).

Visions of Scottish and Catalan independence in Europe 23

Dalle Mulle, Emmanuel and Ivan Serrano (2019). Between a principled and a consequentialist logic: Theory and practice of secession in Catalonia and Scotland. *Nations and Nationalism*, 25 (2): 630–651.

De Vries, Catherine E. (2017). Benchmarking Brexit: How the British decision to leave shapes EU public opinion. *Journal of Common Market Studies*, 55 (s1): 38–53.

De Vries, Catherine E. (2018). *Euroscepticism and the future of European integration*. Oxford: Oxford University Press.

Diez Medrano, Juan (2010). Unpacking European identity. *Politique Européenne*, 30 (1): 45–66.

Dion, Stéphane (2012). Secession and the virtues of clarity. *Ottawa Law Review*, 44 (2): 403–418.

Duerr, Glen M.E. (2015). *Secessionism and the European Union: The future of Flanders, Scotland and Catalonia*. Lanham, MD: Lexington Books.

Elias, Anwen (2008). Whatever happened to the Europe of the Regions? Revisiting the regional dimension of European politics. *Regional & Federal Studies*, 18 (5): 483–492.

Elliot, John (2018). *Scots & Catalans: Union and disunion*. New Haven, CT: Yale University Press.

Eriksen, Erik O. and Fossum, Jon E. (eds) (2002). *Democracy in the European Union: Integration through deliberation?* London: Routledge.

Eurobarometer (2021). *Public opinion in the EU*. Standard Eurobarometer 94. Winter 2020–2021. Available at https://europa.eu/eurobarometer/surveys/detail/2355 (accessed 9 June 2021).

Favell, Adrian (2008). *Eurostars and Eurocities: Free movement and mobility in an integrating Europe*. Oxford: Blackwell Publishing.

Fligstein, Neil (2008). *Euroclash: The EU, European identity, and the future of Europe*. Oxford: Oxford University Press.

Føllesdal, Andreas and Hix, Simon (2006). Why there is a democratic deficit in the EU: A response to Majone and Moravcsik. *Journal of Common Market Studies*, 44 (3): 533–562.

Genschel, Philipp and Jachtenfuchs, Marcus (2016). More integration, less federation: The European integration of core state powers. *Journal of European Public Policy*, 23 (1): 42–59.

Haas, Ernst (1958). *The uniting of Europe: Political, economic, and social forces, 1950–1957*. Stanford, CA: Stanford University Press.

Harteveld, Eelco, van der Meer, Tom and Vries, Catherine E. (2013). In Europe we trust? Exploring three logics of trust in the European Union. *European Union Politics*, 14 (4), 542–565.

Hepburn, Eve (ed.) (2011). *New challenges for stateless nationalist and regionalist parties*. London: Routledge.

Hobolt, Sarah B. and Tilley, James (2016). Fleeing the centre: The rise of challenger parties in the aftermath of the euro crisis. *West European Politics*, 39 (5): 971–991.

24 *Visions of Scottish and Catalan independence in Europe*

Hooghe, Liesbet and Marks, Gary (2004). Does identity or economic rationality drive public opinion on European integration? *PS: Political Science and Politics*, 37 (3): 415–420.

Hooghe, Liesbet and Marks, Gary (2009). A postfunctionalist theory of European integration: From permissive consensus to constraining dissensus. *British Journal of Political Science*, 39 (1): 1–23.

Jolly, Seth K. (2007). The Europhile fringe? Regionalist party support for European integration. *European Union Politics*, 8 (1): 109–130.

Jolly, Seth K. (2015). *The European Union and the rise of regionalist parties.* Ann Arbor: University of Michigan Press.

Jordana, Jacint, Keating, Michael, Marx, Axel and Wouters, Jan (eds) (2019). *Changing borders in Europe: Exploring the dynamics of integration, differentiation and self-determination in the European Union.* London: Routledge.

Keating, Michael (1998). *The new regionalism in Western Europe: Territorial restructuring and political change.* Cheltenham: Edward Elgar Publishing.

Keating, Michael (2001). *Plurinational democracy.* Oxford: Oxford University Press.

Keating, Michael (2019). Is a theory of self-determination possible? *Ethnopolitics*, 18 (3): 315–323.

Keating, Michael, Jordana, Jacint, Marx, Axel and Wouters, Jan (2019). States, sovereignty, borders, self-determination in Europe. In Jacint Jordana, Michael Keating, Axel Marx and Jan Wouters (eds), *Changing borders in Europe: Exploring the dynamics of integration, differentiation and self-determination in the European Union.* London: Routledge.

Kenealy, Daniel (2014). how do you solve a problem like Scotland? A proposal regarding 'internal enlargement'. *Journal of European Integration*, 36 (6): 585–600.

Kornprobst, Markus (2008). *Irredentism in European politics: Argumentation, compromise and norms.* Cambridge: Cambridge University Press.

Kriesi, Hanspeter (2014). The populist challenge. *West European Politics*, 37 (2): 361–378.

Laible, Janet (2008). *Separatism and sovereignty in the new Europe: Party politics and the meanings of statehood in a supranational context.* New York: Palgrave Macmillan.

Liñeira, Robert and Cetrà, Daniel (2015). The independence case in comparative perspective. *The Political Quarterly*, 86 (2): 257–264.

Linz, Juan J. and Stepan, Alfred (1996). *Problems of democractic transition and consolidation.* Baltimore, MD: Johns Hopkins University Press.

MacCormick, Neil (1997). Democracy, subsidiarity, and citizenship in the 'European Commonwealth'. *Law and Philosophy*, 16 (4): 331–356.

Mair, Peter (2013). *Ruling the void: The hollowing of Western democracy.* London: Verso Books.

Majone, Giandomenico (1998). Europe's 'democratic deficit': The question of standards. *European Law Journal*, 4 (1): 5–28.

Manners, Ian (2011). Symbolism in European integration. *Comparative European Politics*, 9 (3): 243–268.

Visions of Scottish and Catalan independence in Europe 25

Marks, Gary, Hooghe, Liesbet and Blank, Kermit (1996). European integration from the 1980s: State-centric v. multi-level governance. *Journal of Common Market Studies*, 34 (3): 341–378.

McNamara, Kathleen R. (2016). *The politics of everyday Europe: Constructing authority in the European Union*. Oxford: Oxford University Press.

McTavish, Duncan and Garnett, Mark (2020). Scottish and UK politics: Convergence and divergence. In Mark Garnett (ed.), *The Routledge handbook of British politics and society*. London: Routledge, 244–257.

Moravcsik, Andrew (1998). *The choice for Europe: Social purpose and state power from Messina to Maastricht*. London: Routledge.

Moravcsik, Andrew (2002). Reassessing legitimacy in the European Union. *Journal of Common Market Studies*, 40 (4): 603–624.

Moreno, Luis (2001). *The federalization of Spain*. London: Frank Cass.

Muro, Diego and Vlaskamp, Martijn (2016). How do prospects of EU membership influence support for secession? A survey experiment in Catalonia and Scotland. *West European Politics*, 39 (6): 1115–1138.

Müller, Jan-Werner (2016). *What is populism?* Philadelphia: University of Pennsylvania Press.

Norman, Ludvig (2017). Defending the European political order: Visions of politics in response to the radical right. *European Journal of Social Theory*, 20 (4): 531–549.

Piris, Jean-Claude (2017a). Political and legal aspects of recent regional secessionist trends in some EU Member States (I). In Carlos Closa (ed.), *Secession from a member state and withdrawal from the European Union: Troubled membership*. Cambridge: Cambridge University Press, 69–87.

Piris, Jean-Claude (2017b). Political and legal aspects of recent regional secessionist trends in some EU Member States (II). In Carlos Closa (ed.), *Secession from a member state and withdrawal from the European Union: Troubled Membership*. Cambridge: Cambridge University Press, 88–105.

Reinikainen, Jouni (2019). What is the democratic approach to plebiscitary secessionism? *Ethnopolitics*, 18 (4): 362–378.

Roeder, Philip G. (2007). *Where nation-states come from: Institutional change in the Age of Nationalism*. Princeton, NJ: Princeton University Press.

Rokkan, Stein and Derek W. Urwin (1983). *Economy, territory, identity: Politics of West European peripheries*. London: SAGE.

Rydgren, Jens (2017). Radical right-wing parties in Europe: What's populism got to do with it? *Journal of Language and Politics*, 16 (4): 485–496.

Scottish National Party (SNP) (2020). *We're asking our friends in Europe to leave a light on for Scotland*. 31 January. Available at www.snp.org/we-are-asking-our-friends-in-europe-to-leave-a-light-on-for-scotland/ (accessed 21 May 2021).

ScotCen Social Research (2020). *Scottish social attitudes 2019: Attitudes to government and political engagement*. Available at www.gov.scot/publications/scottish-social-attitudes-2019-attitudes-government-political-engagement/ (accessed 7 December 2021).

26 *Visions of Scottish and Catalan independence in Europe*

Seubert, Sandra, Eberl, Oliver and van Waarden, Frans (eds) (2018). *Reconsidering EU citizenship: Contradictions and constraints.* Cheltenham: Edward Elgar Publishing.

Sorens, Jason (2012). *Secessionism: Identity, interest, and strategy.* Montreal: McGill-Queen's University Press.

Tilly, Charles (1992). *Coercion, capital, and European states, AD 990–1992.* Oxford: Blackwell.

Van Middelaar, Luuk (2013). *The passage to Europe: How a continent became a union.* New Haven, CT: Yale University Press.

Weiler, Joseph H.H. (1991). The transformation of Europe. *Yale Law Journal,* 100 (8): 2403–2483.

2 Different paths to independence in Europe

By the late 2000s, despite significant differences between them, the Scottish and Catalan pro-independence movements were each reaching critical junctures in their evolution, as they progressed towards presenting their first major bids for statehood. In Scotland, the Scottish National Party (SNP) proceeded to press for a referendum on independence from the UK once it had won control of the Scottish Parliament in the election of May 2011. In Catalonia, Convergència Democràtica de Catalunya (CDC) finally adopted 'a state of our own' as its objective at the 16th party congress in March 2012. In the same year, following the re-election of its leader Artur Mas as the electoral candidate of Convergència i Unió (CiU) – a party federation through which CDC collaborated with the Christian Democrat Unió Democràtica de Catalunya (UDC) until 2015 – different Catalan pro-independence forces began to work together to undertake what would become known as the *Procés*, whereby they would seek to secure independence from Spain. Essentially, at the political level, this meant that CDC, part of UDC and Esquerra Republicana de Catalunya (ERC) worked together in the Catalan Parliament and ultimately presented a successful joint list in the Catalan election of September 2015. Their subsequent coalition Government was able to maintain an absolute majority of the seats so long as it could draw support from the radical anti-capitalist Candidatura d'Unitat Popular (CUP), a locally based grassroots movement which had entered the Catalan Parliament in 2012 and saw its representation grow three years later amid a surge in popular support for independence, much of it mobilized by two burgeoning civil society organizations, the Assemblea Nacional Catalana and Òmnium Cultural.

Focusing on the period from the 1950s to 2010, this chapter maps the historical evolution of visions of 'Europe' and European integration held by Scottish and Catalan pro-independence parties, including

DOI: 10.4324/9781003129028-2

28 *Different paths to independence in Europe*

those regionalist parties whose territorial objectives and goals became secessionist relatively recently. The chapter compares how these parties responded to different developments in the process of European integration as it evolved from the initial community-building phase to periodic enhancement efforts, including the Single European Act and the Treaty on European Union (TEU), as well as looking at party responses to European Community (EC)/European Union (EU) enlargements. Although the relationship of regionally based parties to the EC/EU was never meant to be a one-way traffic, the chapter reflects on how limited the early reactions of European institutions were to the demands made by such parties. They have had to struggle to exert any significant influence on an international organization in which state representation has been privileged and the most persistent debates have been to do with the balance between intergovernmental and supranational decision-making, with the principle of subsidiarity only being applied lower down through the merely advisory input afforded to the Committee of the Regions (CoR), established in 1994 as a result of the TEU, and in relation to the management of regional funding programmes.

The chapter also identifies domestic factors that have driven the evolution of party positioning on European matters, especially in Scotland where there have been greater inter- and intra-party differences on EC/EU membership issues than in Catalonia. The chapter is thus mainly focused on identifying the driving forces and dynamics that have underpinned shifts in visions of European integration held by those parties, as well as the continuities to be found in party outlooks, particularly in Catalonia, notwithstanding more fundamental changes over time in Catalan party attitudes towards independence.

Scottish and Catalan pro-independence parties in a comparative perspective

The background to the political dynamics in the two cases, particularly in terms of the nature of the movements, the strategy of the parties and their attitudes towards Europe and towards independence are rather different. First, the Scottish nationalist movement has been dominated entirely by one party, the SNP, which was founded in 1934, whereas nationalist politics and the wider pro-sovereignty movement in Catalonia have been populated by a number of parties, each with their own patterns of historical evolution, and owing to their associations with civil society, capable of mobilizing vast numbers of people in recent years. The SNP has avoided being challenged electorally by

Different paths to independence in Europe 29

other nationalist parties; it has succeeded as a 'broad church', helped by the fact that it chose to use the word 'national' rather than 'nationalist' when choosing its name. The political dynamics of the Catalan movement have been much more complex, as it is as much an arena of rivalry as well as alliances among several significant parties at any one time; it has seen periods in which factionalism has prospered, at times undermining the unity among pro-independence forces from within.

In addition to sharing a common republican orientation, all sectors of the Catalan independence movement have been *catalanista*, upholding the Catalan language and culture and a distinctive vision of the historical relationship between Catalonia and Spain. However, whereas part of the movement (especially CiU while under the leadership of Jordi Pujol) has gone through periods when it readily accepted Catalonia's constitutional status as an autonomous region of Spain, other parties that are currently making independence claims have pursued federal, confederal or independence agendas for part of, or throughout, their histories. Moreover, while sections of the movement historically have used and accepted the vocabulary of nationalism, in recent years certain activists and parties comprising Catalonia's pro-independence movement have tended to reject the 'nationalist' label and insist that their desire for independence, or for the right of Catalans to decide their own future constitutional status by means of a recognized referendum, stems from an essentially democratic vocation (Amorós interview 2014). Recently, ERC has defined itself as 'Catalonia's major left-wing national party' (ERC n.d.)

Many of the arguments for Catalan autonomy and independence have traditionally been based on a desire to protect and promote the national culture, the language of Catalá being widely spoken (unlike Gaelic in Scotland); only more recently have they been reinforced by the expression of widely held economic grievances against the Spanish state. In contrast, Scottish nationalism has been primarily political in orientation and driven more by socio-economic considerations (Keating 1997). The SNP has not defined Scottish nationalism in linguistic or cultural terms: indeed, it describes Scottish society as multicultural (Laible 2008: 52), whereas Catalan nationalists have tended to be wary of 'multiculturalism' and have prioritized language promotion as a central means to integrate Catalan society when faced with migration from within Spain and abroad. Another contrast is that, while Scotland's relationship to British democracy has seen a lot of historical continuity, Catalonia has had a more limited democratic context in which to develop (Elliot 2018). Even into the current century, Catalan

30 Different paths to independence in Europe

and Spanish outlooks were influenced by historical memories of the long, repressive Francoist era (1939–1976), during which Europe was looked to as an emblem of freedom and democracy. The earliest of the parties that feature in our analysis (UDC and ERC) go back to the early 1930s and the political opportunities afforded by the Second Republic of 1931–1936, but openings for the expression of Catalan nationalism scarcely existed in Catalonia during the long years of authoritarian rule under Franco. During the dictatorship, the movement survived in Catalonia largely at the cultural level, as well as abroad, where Catalan exiles tried to maintain party structures and develop international contacts. CDC, created in 1974, had its origins in the final period of Francoism in crisis.

In relation to Europe, the long-range picture is again very different in Catalonia and Scotland. Although it initially welcomed moves towards cooperation in Western Europe, the SNP remained focused on asserting Scottish sovereignty vis-à-vis the UK. During the EC's infancy, the party was often critical of international organizations such as the Common Market, seeing them as antithetical to its desire for Scottish sovereignty (Newell 1994: 81). It did not come to see the EC as an international context conducive to the satisfaction of SNP ambitions until the late 1970s, when it started moving towards embracing the idea of 'independence in Europe', a shift that was completed in 1988 (Hepburn 2009; Jolly 2015; Jackson 2020). In contrast, in what was historically Spain's most prosperous region, the traditional Catalan project had set out to modernize, democratize and Europeanize Spain rather than seeking to create an independent Catalan state (Dowling 2013: 136).

The process of European integration was widely welcomed in Catalonia from the outset and the Catalanist mood was entirely sympathetic when the European Economic Community (EEC) denied entry to Francoist Spain, for being non-democratic, and proceeded to deny it an association agreement in 1962 (Powell 2015: 7–9). Later, the Generalitat de Catalunya would boast of having an office in Brussels even before democratic Spain's accession in June 1986, and ahead of other Spanish regions (Nagel 2009). As well as being a source of economic opportunities, Europe was seen by Catalans as a de facto ally of the cause of regaining democratic freedoms and rights. Once these were restored in the years following Franco's death in 1975, becoming part of Europe was viewed as a means of safeguarding the fledgling democracy created in 1976–1978. For many Catalans, it was envisaged too as facilitating their ambition to obtain autonomy, initially through the Catalan statute of 1979, and enabling them to safeguard and press

Different paths to independence in Europe 31

for its enhancement thereafter. Even today, with the exception of the anti-capitalist CUP and the far-right Vox, all the significant parties in Catalonia are supportive of the EU.

The other main contrast is that, whereas the SNP has always focused on independence, albeit for many years as a rather distant goal, the larger parties of the Catalan nationalist movement only adopted it as an official objective relatively late in their histories: ERC in 1989, initially as rather a utopian endgame to be achieved in the long term (Carod-Rovira interview 2014) and only as the intended outcome of a roadmap from 2011, under the leadership of Oriol Junqueras; and CDC from 2012, after seeing a strengthening of internal pro-sovereignty currents from the 1990s (Gillespie 2017). Here, the Catalan parties were much closer to mainstream public opinion. After decades of weak support for independence in Scotland, MORI polls found independence to be backed by 14 per cent of the population on the eve of the first referendum on devolution in 1979, which attracted too small a turnout for the outcome to bring the Scotland Act into effect. Support for independence grew in the late 1980s, during the final years of the widely unpopular UK Government of Margaret Thatcher, reaching a peak of 47 per cent in 1998 after the second, this time effective, devolution referendum, but it then varied in the ensuing years before rising to present a strong challenge from 2010 onwards (Ipsos MORI 2012). In Catalonia, support for independence increased from 8 per cent in 1979, when the region formed the basis of one of the new *comunidades autónomas* covering the map of the new Spain, to reach 20 per cent in 1990, but then declined before starting to rise once more in the second half of the 2000s (Balfour and Quiroga 2007: 156). From 1991, Institut de Ciències Polítiques i Socials polls on independence in Catalonia, for or against, put support at between 30 and 40 per cent for two decades (except briefly, at 43 per cent, in 2003), before rising above 40 per cent in 2011 (ICPS n.d.).

However, while it made sense to ask about 'independence, for or against' in view of a possible eventual referendum on the issue, that question failed to elicit a full picture of popular preferences in territorial debates. Centre d'Estudis d'Opinió polls, produced by the Catalan Government, have asked about independence in comparison with other preferences, i.e. for a federal state, an autonomous community or a region, and when the issue was posed in that way support for independence was backed by smaller proportions of the electorate, rising from 13.6 per cent in June 2005 to reach 20.9 per cent in May 2009 and to more than 30 per cent by 2012 (CEO n.d.)

32 *Different paths to independence in Europe*

Early responses to the European integration process

During the early years of European integration, nationalist parties were weak and in no position to play influential roles either in the host states their nations were ruled by or in the European arena. The SNP was completely marginal to a regional party system dominated by the Scottish Labour Party, while ERC and other Catalan parties suffered repression at the hands of the Franco regime. Within the SNP, the aspiration to take part in the process of European integration was mostly held by a few intellectuals, who emphasized the European connections that Scotland had developed traditionally. For most members, independence was such a remote prospect that positioning the party vis-à-vis steps in European integration seemed of little relevance. In any case, there was a widespread belief in the party that the international interests of Scotland could be best served via some form of cooperation between sovereign British nations and/or through the Commonwealth (Laible 2008: 77).

Thus, the European developments leading to the Treaty of Rome were of fairly marginal importance for the SNP, even though it had expressed support for European unity in 1948, subject to it being organized in a federation in which all participating nations would enjoy equal status (Laible 2008: 77). It was only when the state-wide parties of the UK began to debate whether to join the EEC that the SNP began to say more about Europe, owing to the greater urgency of considering how key Scottish interests would be affected by British entry as well as to the way that the UK authorities denied Scotland and Wales any specific structured input in the negotiations on the terms of adhesion. The prospect of being presented with a fait accompli of a British entry on terms inimical to Scottish socio-economic and sectoral interests (notably fisheries) was what led the SNP to speak with a more Eurosceptical voice from the 1960s, yet also to underscore that Scotland needed self-government if it were to have any influence on what happened at the European level (ibid.: 76). As Lynch put it, SNP attitudes to Europe had 'fluctuated between positive attitudes to European integration in the 1940s and 1950s to a mixture of qualified and outright opposition to a politically and economically centralised European Community in the 1960s and 1970s' (2006: 241).

Meanwhile, Catalan nationalists saw European integration as strengthening the democratic forces in Europe, enabling Catalans to 'escape from' or 'bypass' Spain (Dowling 2013: 149). Having been defeated militarily by Franco in the Civil War and with most

Different paths to independence in Europe 33

resistance to his rule suppressed by the late 1940s, Catalan nationalists as well as republicans pinned their hopes for eventual regime change more on shifts in the balance of forces in Europe and internationally than on overthrowing the Spanish regime through domestic efforts. Unable to operate openly as political forces, Catalan nationalists joined associations that were tolerated by Franco; they took part in establishing the European Movement in Catalonia in 1949 and followed the European process closely (de Gispert interview 2014). Surviving supporters of ERC became involved in the Consell Català del Moviment Europeu from the late 1940s and later took part in the Club d'Amics de la Unesco, created in 1960 (Culla i Clarà 2013: 103). Following Franco's signing of a defence treaty with the USA in 1953, a Concordat with the Vatican in 1955 and Spain's admission to the Organisation for Economic Co-operation and Development in 1959, the one gleam of hope for republicans came with the creation of the EEC by a group of Western European democracies and the failure of Spanish regime efforts to obtain an Association Agreement with it in 1962.

Catalonia's historical status as the main engine room of industrialization in Spain had made it confident and ambitious enough to become by far the country's most pro-European region (Smith 2014), and some nationalists made explicit connections between modernization, European integration and regime change. CDC founder Jordi Pujol, who spoke of being personally influenced by Winston Churchill's speech in Zurich in 1946, advocating a Council of Europe, argued that 'Catalonia has not just been a pro-European link for Spain but also a spearhead for Spain in Europe' (1986: 10). His speeches while President of the Catalan Government (1980–2003) demonstrate how, during the early history of CiU, mainstream Catalan nationalism played the role of a regional party within the EC, in which he sought leading roles for Catalonia and Spain alike, in a fruitful Catalan-Spanish-European relationship; this outlook only began to change when Spain's own external relations vision was modified in the direction of Atlanticism under José María Aznar, Spanish Prime Minister between 1996 and 2004 (Pujol 2012: 34). ERC, in the late 20th century a much less influential party, often expressed itself in more unqualified nationalistic terms. In 1993, it described its final objective in the European sphere as being 'a federal Europe based on real nations' (ERC 1993: 95); it wanted to see the disappearance of 'artificial states' such as Spain possessing a 'plurinational' character, whereas CiU still entertained hopes of obtaining further autonomy within the Spanish state.

34 *Different paths to independence in Europe*

Treaty changes, institutional developments and enlargement

Following the nationalist parties' original positioning on European integration, shifts in the evolution of their attitudes were much more evident in the Scottish case than in Catalonia. This was partly a mark of the SNP spending far longer as an opposition party, trying to develop arguments and assume positions designed to enhance its electoral competitiveness and partly of its more critical attitude towards the EC from an early date. The Scottish party did not enter government until 2007, whereas in Catalonia, following the return of democratic elections in 1977, CiU was only out of office for seven years (2003–2010), during which ERC took part in a socialist-led tripartite government committed to an enhancement of the Catalan autonomy statute. Prior to 1977, with no opportunity to compete in elections for four decades dominated by Franco, Catalans had held firm to the idea of Europe even when the institutional model that was developed by the EC diverged considerably from the ideal, more decentralized models of European integration advocated by Catalanist parties. Moreover, with Spain joining the EC later than the UK, the Catalan parties saw less need to adopt official positions on most of the periodic developments in the integration process at the European level. Despite these differences, comparison between the Scottish and Catalan cases is still possible.

The SNP's shift to a more Eurosceptical position in the 1960s had much to do with the accession process of the UK, the early institutional design of the EC as provided for in the Treaty of Rome, the party's international outlook and the logic of electoral competition in Scotland. The UK accession process was perceived negatively by the SNP for two reasons, one being that Scotland had no part in the accession negotiations as a nation (only through the British parties represented at Westminster), and the other being a reaction to centralizing tendencies in the way that the EC was structured (Lynch 2006: 241). The party manifesto for the 1974 general election continued to refer to the EC as 'highly bureaucratic, centralist and undemocratic—remote from the control of ordinary people'. The Common Market was a 'centralist empire' that had fallen well short of party aspirations (Jolly 2015: 114; Laible 2008: 82). Thus, further integration was opposed by the SNP, which also objected that the Community, as a Western European entity, was compounding a Cold War divide that was threatening world peace (Laible 2008: 82). Electoral considerations also influenced SNP positions on Europe in that, early on, the party was keen to differentiate itself from the Labour Party, the

Different paths to independence in Europe 35

leading party in Scotland at the time, which ultimately favoured British membership. Later, its return to a more positive stance was influenced to some degree by an opportunity to differentiate itself from the Scottish Conservatives, as the Tories started to strike more Eurosceptical notes under Thatcher's leadership (Jolly 2015: 114–116).

It took decades for the SNP to arrive at a positive position on the EC through a thorough internal debate. The party's opposition softened somewhat after the UK's membership had been confirmed by the British referendum of 1975, in which the party had formed part of the 'no' camp. Acceptance of the fait accompli then became evident in the slogan 'no voice, no entry', whereby it was not membership per se but rather the manner in which membership had been negotiated that was condemned (Lynch 2006: 241). The SNP now also began to speak of sovereignty in less absolute terms, in view of the progress of European integration and growing global interdependence. In 1976, with Europe not yet a salient ongoing issue for the party, it accepted that nations needed to yield some sovereignty if they wished to promote peace and stability through international collaboration. A further qualification of its opposition was apparent three years later when, in another electoral manifesto, specific aspects of EC policy (such as the threat to Scottish fishing grounds and the way in which agricultural subsidies were being used by other member states) were criticized, rather than the European project itself (Jolly 2015: 114–115).

Shifting to a positive position during the 1980s owed much to developments in European integration that made the EC itself both more desirable and unavoidable for Scottish nationalists. By then, trade integration had intensified, UK ties to Europe had increased and the EC's share of global trade had grown (Laible 2008: 97), besides which the single market was now on the agenda. Moreover, under the presidency of Jacques Delors, the European Commission was presenting the vision of a 'social Europe', something that appealed to the SNP following its journey from a somewhat centrist position in the 1960s towards centre-left politics. Meanwhile, the party's own electoral misfortunes also pushed it towards a pro-European definition, as advocated by a new generation of leaders, notably Alex Salmond, that provided much of the agency that made the underlying driving forces effective. A succession of electoral setbacks had forced even members of the old guard to take a hard look at where the SNP was failing and one of their conclusions was that the party had ignored the existence of growing pro-European sentiments in Scottish society, where support for European integration had risen by 25 per cent between 1979 and 1997 (Jolly 2015: 11). Public opinion polls in 1988 showed that,

36 *Different paths to independence in Europe*

while only one-fifth of Scots supported independence, one-third backed the notion of independence *in Europe* (Newell 1994: 81). Once the latter had been adopted as the SNP's goal, it then proved popular, with the party coming close to winning a second seat in elections to the European Parliament in 1989 (Laible 2008: 113).

Rather than just being a product of electoral calculation, SNP attitudes towards European integration were informed by a changed mindset, cognizant of how enlargements of the EC had brought in a number of smaller nations, whose leaders were reporting positive outcomes from membership and arguing that the compromise on sovereignty was worthwhile: shared sovereignty in an increasingly powerful European organization was giving these countries more international influence than they had possessed alone. The SNP also saw economic benefits in evidence in the smaller states, with even the poorer member states doing well as the structural funds were expanded. Making debatable assumptions about the future of North Sea oil and the amount of access that a new Scottish state would have to its revenues, the SNP claimed that an independent Scotland would be the eighth richest country in the world (Jolly 2015: 117).

The Scottish nationalists were now much more convinced of the benefits of economic integration and indeed saw dangers in an independent Scotland *not* being part of the internal market (Newell 1994: 82). They were even open to the possibility of joining the future eurozone, although they had ongoing concerns about it. They remained strongly critical of centralization and would continue to defend intergovernmental approaches to European decision-making and confederalism (Lynch 2006: 241) but saw more centralized decision-making at the European level as inevitable given the momentous changes being contemplated at this stage of European integration. Despite their longstanding concerns about supranationalism, some reassurance was provided by further enlargement perspectives: as former leader Gordon Wilson had said of the EC, 'the bigger it gets, the looser it becomes' (Laible 2008: 108). In any case, centralization was something the SNP could only hope to have a say over through securing independent representation for Scotland.

By adopting the slogan 'Independence in Europe', the SNP also aimed to reassure Scottish voters that separation from the UK involved less risk of adverse economic consequences than straightforward national independence would, although much would depend on negotiating satisfactory terms of entry and on how the creation of a new national border would leave the question of North Sea oil. From the 1990s, while looking to accede through a successful negotiation of

Different paths to independence in Europe 37

points around Scotland's special national interests, the party maintained that Scotland would be allowed to remain in the EU following independence (Jolly 2015: 116). Contrary to some expectations (Hepburn 2010: 20), the progress of European integration did not lead the SNP to curb its ambitions for independence; indeed, the party continued to decide positions on Europe from the perspective of its strategic thinking on independence. Unlike CiU, at no time did the Scottish party resign itself to playing the role of a regionalist party and it was immediately sceptical about the CoR when it was established in 1994. Since this would not give Scotland a role in EU decision-making, the SNP's desire for independence was if anything strengthened by this development (Laible 2008: 113). In the European Parliament, the party showed no interest in alignment with regionalist parties, preferring to place itself initially (from 1979 to 1989) in the same political group as the French Gaullists and the Irish Fianna Fáil.

In Catalonia, meanwhile, the context in which Catalan nationalists reacted to the evolution of the EU was very different, especially regarding variables such as the existence of authoritarian regime change/continuity and the timing and extent of devolution. While the UK enjoyed decades of ongoing institutional stability, Spain in the late 1970s underwent a transition to liberal democracy negotiated by government and opposition elites following decades of Francoist authoritarian centralism. This backcloth made many Catalan nationalists, as well as others who ideally wanted to see more radical change, moderate their demands for fear of provoking a reactionary backlash through a military coup (as was attempted by Spanish army and Guardia Civil elements in February 1981). Devolution was initiated in Spain some 20 years before there was sufficient support for it to be introduced in a Scottish referendum and the reach of the powers devolved to Catalonia was greater, although less than those negotiated by Madrid with the representatives of Euskadi and Navarra, who were able to cite historical precedents in the Basque *fueros*[1] to argue for a measure of fiscal sovereignty (Gray 2015: 66–68).

Although the introduction of devolution did not reduce the level of support for independence immediately or permanently, the latter did fall from the late 1980s until the great recession began in 2008, that is, it declined once Spain had begun to experience economic success and international influence under socialist governments headed by Felipe González. Towards the end of the 20th century, there was a widespread perception throughout Spain that accession to the EC in 1986 had been greatly beneficial, with the country under González proceeding to 'punch above its weight' in Europe, and Catalonia under

38 *Different paths to independence in Europe*

Pujol publicly welcoming and taking full advantage of the new opportunities that 'Europe' afforded to Catalan business and citizens.

For decades, the dominant party in Catalan politics, CiU, expressed no criticisms of the EC and collaborated pragmatically with Spanish governments, indeed upholding them through the votes of its Members of Parliament in Madrid on occasions when the leading Spanish party found itself lacking an overall majority in the Spanish Congreso de los Diputados (Congress of Deputies). These included the Partido Socialista Obrero Español (PSOE) in 1993–1996 and the Partido Popular (PP) in 1996–2000. CDC 'defined itself as an unconditional supporter of the process of the integration of Spain in European institutions, of the consolidation of the European Union, and of the incorporation of Spain in the leading group of countries as monetary union [proceeded]' (Marcet and Argelaguet 1998: 76–77). Notwithstanding his role as a major promoter of the 'Europe of the Regions' idea, Pujol avoided confrontation between this concept and 'the Europe of the nation-states' (ibid.); instead, he looked to both levels of governance to advance the cause of European integration. Even in retirement, when voicing disappointment with the state of Europe in 2013, he saw this as a 'collective' failure by Europeans, rather than something that could be attributed purely to the recent increase in member state dominance in respect of EU decision-making (Pujol interview 2013). Throughout his active political career and before he eventually expressed support for independence, Pujol believed in gradually attaining more autonomy for Catalonia in a regionalized Europe that would eventually supersede the Spanish state (Barberà and Barrio 2006: 116). Meanwhile CDC's coalition partner in CiU, UDC, envisioned a federal Europe with clear delimitation between European, national and regional levels of governance (Guibernau 2004: 140–141).

Pujol's governments in the 1980s and 1990s not only accepted EC/ EU regionalism but set out to actively shape it (Crameri 2008: 19), partly through the CoR and by building a network of partnerships with similarly prosperous European regions. As a mark of Catalan success in Europe, the Catalan leader became President of the Assembly of European Regions in 1992–1996. Later, however, Pujol expressed criticism of the CoR's limitations, having experienced personally how the stronger regions were often frustrated by alliances between weaker regions and local administrations (Nagel 2009), the latter's very presence contradicting the notion of a 'Europe of the Regions' that CiU wished to see at this time.

The eventual reservations expressed about the CoR did not detract from CiU's ongoing support for the process of European integration, within which other useful opportunities for Catalonia were perceived. By

Different paths to independence in Europe 39

the start of the 21st century, even with CiU losing ground electorally, it still accepted the parameters of the Spanish model of regional autonomy. Its territorial agenda focused on negotiating an enhancement of Catalonia's regional statute and using the TEU provision to secure representation in Spanish delegations to EU institutions whenever issues of regional competence were being decided. Significantly, CiU's demand for direct involvement in the process of defining Spain's position on EU policies was lobbied for in the name of the autonomous communities in general rather than for Catalonia alone (CiU 2004: 372).

ERC's positioning was distinct yet similar to that of CiU. The Left Republicans' support for European integration was not disturbed by the party's shift towards the goal of independence in the late 1980s. The party had voted for the Catalan statute of autonomy in the referendum of 1979, for pragmatic reasons and from a gradualist perspective of eventually obtaining its enhancement, but formally adopted independence as its goal in 1989 after several years of electoral decline and following the entry of young activists into the party from smaller, more radical parties. ERC's electoral recovery was confirmed in the Catalan parliamentary elections of 1992, a year in which it also changed its statutes to place emphasis on independence being sought for all the so-called Catalan Lands, not just the autonomous community of Catalonia in Spain. Its vision now extended to all the Catalan-speaking territories (particularly French and Spanish Catalonia, the region of Valencia and the Balearic Islands) creating their own state within a broader European framework. It thus combined advocacy of the 'territorial unity' of the areas of Catalan linguistic tradition with an underlying commitment to European integration, while seeking democratic reform of the EU to empower citizens (Marcet and Argelaguet 1998: 83).

A further shift occurred in 1996 when a new leadership under Josep-Lluís Carod-Rovira emerged with an agenda of seeking to make ERC the leading force on the Catalan left and open to an alternative party alignment to its existing one with CiU (Culla i Clarà 2013: 465–476). The commitment to independence, seen at this time as a long term-goal, was played down owing to ERC's new interest in working with the Partit dels Socialistes de Catalunya, affiliated to the PSOE, and the post-communist, eco-socialist Iniciativa per Catalunya, both of which advocated an enhanced Catalan statute and either a federal or confederal reorganization of Spain but were decidedly opposed to independence. Despite the potential constraint that collaboration with such partners would entail, the Left Republicans aspired to lead a coalition with them, committed to holding a referendum in which the

40 *Different paths to independence in Europe*

question of independence and perhaps a federalist alternative might be voted on. ERC's readiness to compromise, informed by electoral considerations, came accompanied by a toning down of the vision of uniting the 'Catalan Lands' in favour of pragmatic acceptance that an enhancement of autonomy might have to come initially in the region of Catalonia in Spain, although as a movement it remained organized on a wider territorial basis.

In terms of party discourse, ERC differed from CiU over the question of independence and was quicker to discard the model of a 'Europe of the Regions' and to express disappointment over the CoR. Reacting to the reality of what had been created, Carod-Rovira dismissed the notion of a Europe of the Regions as a 'great utopia', and his party began calling instead for a 'Europe of the Peoples' (Guibernau 2004: 94–95). Then, as it moved to the left, ERC started to talk about the empowerment of 'citizens' as being essential to any European democratizing undertaking. The party's central concern was with finding a way into government after playing such a marginal role for so long, yet even while still out of office, ERC had become more responsive to European and global developments by this time. The ending of the Cold War encouraged a belief that national self-determination might now be possible even in the European context. Although the party still viewed the European project as far from ideal in institutional terms, belonging to the EU was infinitely preferable to accepting US domination in a prospective 'New World Order' (Guibernau 2004: 94). ERC still viewed independence in a vague, utopian way and as a long-term goal (Carod-Rovira interview 2014).

Events such as the independence of the Baltic countries from the Soviet Union and the disintegration of Yugoslavia stimulated hope of statehood for Catalonia and led to pressures within nationalist parties for new territorial formulations, especially from their youth sections, but the responses made on paper by nationalist parties tended to amount at most to demands for shared sovereignty, as in the Barcelona Declaration of 1989, or a confederal relationship to Spain, rather than separation; they have been likened to 'smoke' (Caminal i Badia 2001: 154), which cleared without leaving immediate practical outcomes in terms of transitioning away from the politics of regional autonomy within Spain.

The debate on a Constitution for Europe

The positioning of the Scottish and Catalan parties in the European constitutional debate in the early 2000s deserves special attention since this initiative aiming at deeper political integration raised fundamental

Different paths to independence in Europe 41

issues of sovereignty. The opportunity to join the debate, albeit from the margins of the European Convention, in which CoR representatives enjoyed only observer status, provided a stimulus to clarify what kind of 'Europe' the nationalist parties desired and to express their reservations about member state dominance of the constitutional debate, which Pujol's last government tried to counter through mobilizing Catalan civil society organizations as well as parties. In an attempt to feed proposals into the official EU process devised to draft a European Constitution, Pujol's final government set up a 'Catalan Convention for the Debate on the Future of the EU' and he had taken 80 proposals emanating from participating civil society associations to Brussels in February 2003, representing the fruit of a year's deliberations. The proposals partly set out views on how to strengthen EU institutions and deepen European integration, as well as presenting specific national demands, both political and cultural. Ideas included an enhancement of the EU status of those regions in member states that possessed legislative capacity, rather than merely being administrative units, and also of the status of minority languages such as Catalan within the EU (Nagel 2009).

Scottish nationalist objections to the draft treaty proved to be more fundamental than those of CiU. The SNP's tone was critical throughout the constitutional debate and its response to the exercise has been interpreted as evidence of a growing Euroscepticism in the party at this time (Hepburn 2010: 200), seen especially in its threat to vote against the text if the UK decided to hold a referendum on the issue, an idea that was eventually abandoned in 2005 following rejection of the Treaty establishing a Constitution for Europe in popular referendums held in France and the Netherlands (it was nonetheless supported in an earlier referendum held in Spain). The SNP's 'scepticism' did not involve questioning the party's underlying support for EU membership but did reflect concerns about the emergence of an 'EU super-state' centred around the institutions in Brussels, which was seen as detrimental to Scottish autonomy within the UK. Besides seeing the draft as an obstacle to Scotland being allowed to exercise self-determination, the SNP expressed worries about the extent of further economic integration: ideally it wanted to see fishing removed from the areas of EU competence, while looking ahead it was opposed to the Europeanization of natural resources and taxation (Jolly 2007: 123, 2015: 117–118; Hepburn 2010: 79, 87).

CiU started out with a much more broadly pro-European mindset; indeed, it was judged by academic experts to have been the most pro-EU of all the regionalist parties in the EC/EU between 1984 and 2006

42 *Different paths to independence in Europe*

(Jolly 2015: 98). The creation of a Catalan convention shows that it wanted to participate constructively and not dwell on the shortcomings it saw in the way the proposed Constitutional Treaty was drafted. That its senior partner, CDC, eventually came very close to calling for a 'no' vote in the referendum that Spain held in February 2005 demonstrated not only the party's strong sense of frustration over the way in which its proposals were ignored by the European Convention despite a year of civil society debate in Catalonia, but also the effects of underlying, more structural influences informing party behaviour. One of these was the emergence of concerns about Catalonia being a net contributor to the EU budget, a development that occurred in conjunction with a growing awareness of a trend whereby the region had been slipping further behind Madrid in economic strength (Dowling 2013: 136, 144–145); the other was intense inter-party competition between CiU and ERC, once the former found itself in opposition from 2003, after decades in office (Elias 2015; Gillespie 2017). Neither party wished to appear as a more compromising champion of Catalan interests than the other.

After CiU lost power in 2003, CDC (now led by Artur Mas) was subject to strong pressure from activists to pursue a more sovereignty-oriented course. ERC, which had agreed to join a socialist-led tripartite coalition headed by Pasqual Maragall, was meanwhile swept by rank and file determination to resist unprincipled party compromises with its new partners on the left that might rebound to CiU's electoral advantage. By paying no heed to the Catalan proposals, the draft treaty produced by the European Convention provoked widespread opposition within CDC, whereas its more tightly controlled partner, UDC, saw in the draft certain 'positive' aspects, although it recognized that Catalonia's identity as a European nation was not being recognized. UDC argued that advocacy of a 'no' vote in Spain – the first member state to hold a referendum on the issue – would entail alignment with Eurosceptics and 'mean paralysis, or even regression in the process of European construction' (CiU 2004: 371; *El País* 7 September 2004).

Attempts by Artur Mas to tone down CDC's criticism of the proposed Constitution Treaty were defeated at a party congress in October 2004, which voted by 604 to 31 with 67 abstentions to reject and campaign against the document unless it was modified to recognize Catalan as an official language of the EU and guaranteed an institutional presence for Catalonia in EU bodies (*ABC* 3 October 2004). This put the onus on the new Spanish Prime Minister, the socialist José Luis Rodríguez Zapatero to deliver on his recent general election

Different paths to independence in Europe 43

promise of a more inclusive style of governance by (among other things) acting in recognition of the nationally plural (*plurinacional*) character of Spain (Field 2010). While deciding to modify the composition of Spain's representation in the Council of the EU, the Spanish Government under Zapatero asked for EU recognition of all four of Spain's official languages and for greater use of them in respect of official documentation and communications between EU citizens and EU institutions. The idea of Catalan becoming an official or working language of the EU was rejected, but the Council agreed to make it a language of communication and (to a more limited extent) documentation. In fact, resistance by the European People's Party over the use of Catalan was to persist in the European Parliament, but at the time there seemed to be just enough achievement for Mas to go back to his party and ensure that there would be CDC support and hence CiU unity behind the 'yes' vote in the Spanish referendum (*La Vanguardia* 6 January 2005, 4 July 2006; *Avui* 14 June 2005).

Meanwhile, ERC, together with its tripartite coalition partner Iniciativa per Catalunya Verds (ICV, an alliance between IC and a Catalan Green party), called for a 'no' vote. The party was in favour of a 'European Constitution of the People and the Nations' but felt that the draft Constitutional Treaty had been produced in an undemocratic fashion (ERC 2004). ERC criticisms of the draft constitution were that it had failed to deliver on social issues, recognize the national diversity of the EU, accept the right to self-determination, give representation in decision-making to stateless nations, accept Catalan as an official language or strengthen the European Parliament (ERC 2005).

Thus, the pattern of Catalan political action in the Spanish referendum in 2005 on the European Constitution was for the more conservative, Catholic sector of the nationalist movement, UDC, to remain broadly supportive of the latest European integration initiative. Meanwhile, the more liberal, secular CDC expressed its opposition to some aspects of the initiative and eventually decided only to rally behind what it saw as the positive elements, thus continuing to position itself in the mainstream integrationist camp, while ERC acted on a more doctrinaire basis in calling for a 'no' vote, based on substantive issues, despite making it clear that it nonetheless favoured 'more Europe' of a different kind.

Neither the overwhelming support for the proposed Constitutional Treaty in the Spanish Congress of Deputies (332 out of 350 members) nor the fact that the referendum was non-binding encouraged public engagement in the referendum debate (Torreblanca 2005), but there was much more intervention by cultural and other associations in

44 *Different paths to independence in Europe*

Catalonia than elsewhere in Spain and there the frustrating campaign around the use of Catalan within the EU undoubtedly fuelled a growing belief among CDC activists that Catalonia needed a state of its own if it was to secure its cultural and political objectives in Europe. In Catalonia, the 'no' response to the proposed Constitution (28 per cent) was higher than across Spain as a whole (17 per cent), although it was higher still in the Basque communities (34 per cent in Euskadi, 29 per cent in Navarra). It would be simplistic to see this as evidence of Euroscepticism, given that the more critical forces all advocated for a reformed EU and viewed the European obstacles to the realization of their objectives as secondary to the political battle within the member state: it was the centre-periphery tensions within Spain that were seen as primarily driving the desire for more autonomy (Gillespie 2015).

Evolving and contrasting independence claims in Scotland and Catalonia

This chapter has examined how the positions of the Scottish and Catalan nationalist parties evolved over the question of Europe between the 1950s and the early 2000s, as the European integration process developed as a context with growing impact. These positions have not been arrived at simply through party appraisals of the extent to which the evolving EC/EU has matched their ideals of international organization, in terms of structures and values. Although this has been one criterion for evaluation, changes in party discourse and visions have been influenced too in the long term by their recognition, especially on the part of the SNP following the creation of the EEC, of the growing importance of European integration for their national community, both due to eventual host state accession and the EC/EU's growing international importance during this period. What primarily led nationalists in Catalonia and Scotland to embrace Europe in the post-Second World War period was the calculation that this was the main international body with which involvement would help them to assert autonomy (and some degree of sovereignty) from their host state.

The evolving relationship between nationally based region and member state remained the key arena for nationalist party activity, but with 'Europe' featuring increasingly prominently in the background and later to be deemed a potentially decisive factor once Scottish and Catalan parties began to press sovereignty claims and perceive independence to be a real possibility in the not too distant future. In one

Different paths to independence in Europe 45

way or another, parties seeking to speak on behalf of the stateless nations saw Europe as playing a crucial part in enabling them to strengthen the positions of Scotland and Catalonia vis-à-vis their host state, even though the EC/EU remained decisively dominated by its member states.

Generalization, however, can only be taken so far, one major reason being the qualitative differences that existed between the Catalan and Scottish parties during this period over the way in which they viewed sovereignty. The SNP has always been committed to independence, albeit with a perspective of wishing to cooperate with the rest of the UK following the achievement of statehood, whereas for decades the mainstream Catalan nationalist parties, and especially those forming CiU, were content to operate either through Spain's system of autonomous regions (i.e. a strongly decentralized unitary state) or a proposed federal alternative to be achieved via a reform of the Spanish Constitution. Along with more deeply rooted historical reasons for these contrasting orientations, what made a major difference was the earlier arrival of devolved government in Catalonia, the immediate election to office of CiU and its long political reign in the 1980s and 1990s. While the SNP went through decades as a minority party, forever in opposition, CiU was repeatedly triumphant in Catalan regional elections and was thus able to use public office as a basis for proactive interventions at the European level, where it developed a long-term *pujolista* strategy of engagement. At times, it was able also to use its presence in the Spanish Congress of Deputies to extract more resources for Catalonia or other concessions from minority governments in Madrid in return for helping them to achieve a parliamentary majority.

Meanwhile, it proved adept at operating in the EC/EU, not only through Catalonia's regional governmental activity, which extended to 'external relations', but also through the strong presence of Catalans working in European institutions, including people in quite senior positions in the Commission, often in areas of special interest such as Mediterranean policy. CiU did not perceive of any key EC/EU economic policies as being detrimental to Catalonia, unlike the SNP in respect of the Common Fisheries Policy. The balance of membership for Catalans seemed to be so overwhelmingly positive that CiU (and to some extent ERC) rarely expressed their views on the shortcomings of European institutional arrangements, for within the EC/EU they always perceived some positive developments to be taking place, particularly periodic enhancements of the powers of the European Parliament. By forming joint electoral lists negotiated with Basque and

46 *Different paths to independence in Europe*

Galician nationalist parties in European elections, CiU and ERC gained direct representation there, even though Spain formed a single constituency and nationalist demands for Catalonia to be represented separately fell on deaf ears.

Changes in party discourse on 'Europe' have been much more evident in the history of the SNP than in the Catalan case. With the important exception of CDC's tense debate over the proposed European Constitution, Catalonia saw neither internal disagreements over Europe nor fundamental changes of attitude towards the EC/EU, although nationalist party positions have evolved in relation to the model of European integration, initially embracing yet sooner or later dismissing the concept of a 'Europe of the Regions', as it failed to materialize or develop in the way the nationalists wanted. For the Catalan parties, the introduction of direct elections to the European Parliament in 1979 certainly provided a spur to addressing current EC/EU issues more specifically, since parties needed to produce manifestos for such events, but even then the task did not cause major internal debates. In contrast, from earlier on, the SNP shifted between more positive and more negative positions on the EC/EU itself and in the process underwent years of internal discussion and reconsideration before eventually a tipping point came in the late 1980s in the building of a consensus for a more positive, stable position, facilitated by changes in the party leadership. In Scotland, where the SNP was a marginal electoral competitor for so long, manoeuvring to gain advantage within the Scottish party system and to draw closer to broader sectors of public opinion were key considerations behind modifications in party position, reflecting the importance of divisions over Europe in both Scotland and the wider UK. Electoral calculations played a big role in finally bringing the SNP to what proved to be a settled formulation of 'independence in Europe', in contrast to Catalonia where the competitive parties, even the People's Party, were all pro-European, at least until the PP began to win Spanish general elections in 1996, after which overriding Atlanticist ambitions became more evident in the Spanish Governments under José María Aznar.

In Catalonia and in Spain in general, where debates about 'Europe' were so interwoven with a desire to sustain the post-Franco liberalization and democratization processes, the societal consensus over EC/EU membership found expression in all the mainstream parties for decades. Although Zapatero failed to obtain satisfaction from the EU over the request for Catalan to be made an official language, there was nevertheless a Spanish Government that made use of TEU provisions to enable regional representatives to join Spanish delegations to the

Different paths to independence in Europe 47

Council of the EU when matters pertaining to policy competences of Spain's autonomous regions were being discussed. Nothing comparable was evident in the Scottish case, where SNP claims about the UK Government's failure to represent the economic interests of Scotland in the EC/EU were a constant refrain in Scottish independence claims.

While the above discussion has brought out some definite limits to the comparability of the Catalan and Scottish cases, it has identified a number of factors behind both continuity and change that will be addressed in the ensuing chapters. How powerful have the historical continuities proved to be as we have moved into the 21st century and pro-independence parties have become more challenging for the EU and its member states? This development has certainly obliged the EU to react more to those speaking in the name of stateless nations, attempting to define a clear position vis-à-vis regional secessionism in the EU, yet not really settling the issue convincingly, once and for all. Have party positions on EU membership and European integration become more settled over time? Do changes in attitudes towards 'Europe' still have so much to do with domestic factors, or has the existence of more interactive dynamics made Scottish and Catalan positions more reactive to official EU positioning on the independence challenges?

While addressing these questions, our analysis indicates that we will also need to focus on political divergence within Scotland and Catalonia on European issues and how this has impacted on the dynamics of party competition therein. Finally, we should consider whether the cases have become more comparable through the pro-independence parties having reached a point where they could actually pose independence as a real possibility, in Scotland through a negotiated process leading to the referendum in 2014 and in Catalonia through the political confrontation over the legitimacy of the unconstitutional 'referendum' of 2017. In some respects, the analysis in this chapter suggests some signs of increased comparability, both in the shift in emphasis of CDC and ERC towards sovereignty and independence politics and in economic themes becoming more prominent in Catalan arguments for a change in the political status quo. Yet some qualitative differences between the two cases may remain constant, in particular the singularly important cultural dimension to the Catalan case, which may in the future have some bearing on the possibilities of eventual political compromises being reached by the actors involved in disputes in the sphere of territorial politics.

48 *Different paths to independence in Europe*

Note

1 Medieval charters that were recognized by the Crown during certain periods of Spain's history.

References

Balfour, Sebastian and Quiroga, Alejandro (2007). *The reinvention of Spain: Nation and identity since democracy.* Oxford: Oxford University Press.

Barberà, Òscar and Astrid Barrio (2006). Convergencia i Unió: From stability to decline? In Lieven De Winter, Margarita Gómez-Reino and Peter Lynch (eds), *Autonomist parties in Europe: Identity politics and the revival of the territorial cleavage.* Vol. 1. Barcelona: Institut de Ciències Polítiques i Socials.

Barrio, Astrid and Barberà, Òscar (2011). Convergència i Unió. In Anwen Elias and Filippo Tronconi (eds), *From protest to power: Autonomist parties and the challenge of representation.* Vienna: Braumüller.

Caminal i Badia, Miquel (2001). El pujolisme i la ideologia nacionalista de Convergència Democràtica de Catalunya. In Juan B. Culla i Clarà (ed.), *El pal de paller: Convergència Democràtica de Catalunya, 1974–2000.* Barcelona: Pòrtic.

Centre d'Estudis d'Opinió (CEO) (n.d.). *Baròmetre.* Available at https://ceo.gencat.cat/ca/barometre/ (accessed 25 August 2021).

Convergència i Unió (CiU) (2004). *Programa electoral de Convergència i Unió: Elecciones a Cortes Generales.* Barcelona: CiU.

Crameri, Kathryn (2008). *Catalonia: National identity and cultural policy, 1980–2003.* Cardiff: University of Wales Press.

Culla i Clarà, Juan B. (2013). *Esquerra Republicana de Catalunya, 1931–2012: Una història política.* Barcelona: La Campana.

Dowling, Andrew (2013). *Catalonia since the Spanish Civil War: Reconstructing the nation.* Eastbourne: Sussex University Press.

Elias, Anwen (2015). Catalan independence and the challenge of credibility: The causes and consequences of Catalan nationalist parties' strategic behaviour. In Richard Gillespie and Caroline Gray (eds), *Contesting Spain? The dynamics of nationalist movements in Catalonia and the Basque Country.* London: Routledge.

Elliot, John (2018). *Scots and Catalans: Union and disunion.* New Haven, CT: Yale University Press.

Esquerra Republicana de Catalunya (ERC) (n.d). *Esquerra's main ideological foundations.* Available at https://en.esquerra.cat/en/esquerra-republicana -ideology-ideological-foundations (accessed 25 August 2021).

Esquerra Republicana de Catalunya (ERC) (1993). *Programa electoral, Eleccions a les Corts espanyoles, Pels Catalans, per Catalunya. Cap a la Independència. Eleccions a les Corts espanyoles.* Available at www.esquerra.cat/uploads/20171218/e1993_programaLR.pdf (accessed 9 June 2021).

Different paths to independence in Europe 49

Esquerra Republicana de Catalunya (ERC) (2004). *Programa, Eleccions al Parlament Europeu.* Available at www.esquerra.cat/uploads/20171218/eu2004_programa.pdf (accessed 9 June 2021).

Esquerra Republicana de Catalunya (ERC) (2005). *Per moltes raons, aquesta Constitució no. Argumentari.* Barcelona: Esquerra Republicana de Catalunya.

Field, Bonnie C. (ed.) (2010). *Spain's 'Second Transition'? The Socialist Government of José Luis Rodríguez Zapatero.* London: Routledge.

Gillespie, Richard (2015). Between accommodation and contestation: The political evolution of Basque and Catalan nationalism. *Nationalism and Ethnic Politics,* 21 (1): 3–23.

Gillespie, Richard (2017). The contrasting fortunes of pro-sovereignty currents in Basque and Catalan nationalist parties: PNV and CDC compared. *Territory, Politics, Governance,* 5 (4): 406–424.

Gray, Caroline (2015). A fiscal path to sovereignty? The Basque Economic Agreement and nationalist politics. *Nationalism and Ethnic Politics,* 21 (1): 63–82.

Guibernau, Montserrat (2004). *Catalan nationalism: Francoism, transition and democracy.* London: Routledge.

Hepburn, Eve (2009). Degrees of independence: SNP thinking in an international context. In Gary Hassam (ed.), *The modern SNP: From protest to power.* Edinburgh: Edinburgh University Press.

Hepburn, Eve (2010). *Using Europe: Territorial party strategies in a multi-level system.* Manchester: Manchester University Press.

Institut de Ciències Polítiques i Socials (ICPS) (n.d.). *Sondeig d'Opinió Catalunya: Base de dades integrada 1991–2019.* Available at www.icps.cat/recerca/sondeigs-i-dades/basedadesintegrada (accessed 25 August 2021).

Ipsos MORI (2012). *35 years of Scottish attitudes towards independence.* Available at www.ipsos.com/ipsos-mori/en-uk/35-years-scottish-attitudes-towards-independence (accessed 25 August 2021).

Jackson, Ben (2020). *The case for Scottish independence: A history of nationalist political thought in modern Scotland.* Cambridge: Cambridge University Press.

Jolly, Seth K. (2007). The Europhile fringe? Regionalist party support for European integration. *European Union Politics,* 8 (1): 109–130.

Jolly, Seth K. (2015). *The European Union and the rise of regionalist parties.* Ann Arbor: University of Michigan Press.

Keating, Michael (1997). Stateless nation-building: Quebec, Catalonia and Scotland in the changing state system. *Nations and nationalism,* 3 (4): 689–717.

Laible, Janet (2008). *Separatism and sovereignty in the new Europe: Party politics and the meanings of statehood in a supranational context.* New York: Palgrave Macmillan.

Lynch, Peter (2006). The Scottish National Party: The long road from marginality to blackmail and coalition potential. In Lieven De Winter, Margarita Gómez-Reino and Peter Lynch (eds), *Autonomist parties in Europe:*

50 *Different paths to independence in Europe*

Identity politics and the revival of the territorial cleavage. Vol. 1. Barcelona: Institut de Ciències Polítiques i Socials.

Marcet, Juan and Argelaguet, Jordi (1998). Nationalist parties in Catalonia: Convergència Democràtica de Catalunya and Esquerra Republicana. In Lieven De Winter and Huri Tursan (eds), *Regionalist parties in Western Europe.* London: Routledge.

Nagel, Klaus-Jürgen (2009). *The nationalism of stateless nations and Europe: The Catalan case.* Political Theory Working Paper, no. 6. Grup de Recerca en Teoria Política. Barcelona: Universitat Pompeu Fabra.

Newell, James L. (1994). The Scottish National Party: An overview. In Lieven De Winter and Daniel-Loius Seiler (eds), *Non-state wide parties in Europe.* Barcelona: Institut de Ciències Polítiques i Socials.

Payne, Stanley G. (1987). *The Franco regime, 1936–1975.* Madison: University of Wisconsin Press.

Powell, Charles (2015). *The long road to Europe: Spain and the European Community, 1957–1986.* Working Paper, June. Madrid: Real Instituto Elcano.

Pujol, Jordi (1986). *Catalunya i Europa.* Barcelona: Generalitat de Catalunya.

Pujol, Jordi (2012). *El caminante frente al desfiladero.* Barcelona: Destino.

Smith, Ángel. (2014). *The origins of Catalan nationalism, 1770–1898.* Basingstoke: Palgrave Macmillan.

Torreblanca, José I. (2005). Spain's referendum on the European Constitution: A double disappointment. *Revistas ARI*, 27.

3 Catalan independence and European integration
From idealism to realism?

Since the turn of the century, Catalonia has presented Spain with its greatest constitutional challenge, going well beyond the push for shared sovereignty represented by the Ibarretxe Plan in the Basque Country during the early 2000s. It has involved peaceful mass, indeed massive, mobilization and a strong element of civil society action bringing pressure from below, whereas the Basque process unfolded essentially through political elite initiatives, with action by Euskadi ta Azkatasuna (Basque Homeland and Liberty) at that time still a major constraint on civil society expression (Gillespie 2017). As well as being unprecedented for Spain, the Catalan challenge has been a first for Western Europe, for the Catalan *Procés* saw the first *unilateral* push for statehood in defiance of both constitutional obstacles and ultimately the police action that Spain used in seeking to frustrate it. Even after it suffered a reverse in late 2017 through the temporary suspension of Catalan autonomy and the imprisonment of leading figures, Catalonia continued to present a challenge by giving pro-independence parties a majority of the seats in the Catalan Parliament.

During the past 10–15 years pro-independence parties have made strategic efforts to 'internationalize the Catalan conflict' and most have viewed Europe and the European Union (EU) as potential game-changers in an attempt to alter the balance of forces between those seeking a vote on Catalan national self-determination and the defenders of Spanish sovereignty. This chapter looks at the discourse and claims of the pro-independence forces and why most of them have considered 'Europe' a potential asset in the pursuit of their goal. It examines the way in which party discourses changed as the EU disappointed their early hopes by describing the Catalan challenge as a matter for Spain to resolve, rather than being something for the Union to become involved in. It considers whether European responses have

DOI: 10.4324/9781003129028-3

52 *Catalonia*

bred Euroscepticism and finds that they have led to a more questioning yet still essentially pro-European discourse on the part of representatives of mainstream pro-independence parties.

Discourse of the independence movement on the EU and European integration

The year 2010 was a critical one for the rise of the independence movement, as this was when the ruling by Spain's Constitutional Court on key elements of Catalonia's enhanced autonomy statute of 2006 finally put paid to efforts to achieve official recognition of the region's status as a nation, enhanced political powers and more advantageous financial arrangements. In the words of *Financial Times* international affairs editor David Gardner, the court ruling 'eviscerated' the reform of the 1979 autonomy statute that socialist and nationalist parties had agreed upon and which had been approved, after amendment, by the Spanish Parliament (*Financial Times* 25 October 2012). This gave rise to a qualitative leap in the level of mass mobilization, as civil society organizations grew and began to help to shape the political agenda through their influence on the parties that favoured some degree of sovereignty for Catalonia and a more bilateral relationship with the Spanish state.

Back in 2005, associations such as Òmnium Cultural, Sobirania i Progrés, Sobirania i Justícia and Decidem! had formed a Plataforma pel Dret de Decidir which proceeded to hold its first demonstration in February 2006, using the slogan 'We are a nation and we have the right to decide' (Strubell 2013). This activity attracted people who had been disappointed by the amendments accepted by sovereignty-seeking parties to secure approval of the 2006 autonomy statute by the Spanish Parliament and by the way in which, following the global financial crisis and ensuing recession, the existing regional funding system and pattern of state investment were judged to be serving Catalonia relatively poorly in comparison with many other regions of Spain (Gray 2020: 47–59). In search of wider public support, most of those seeking Catalan independence would continue to emphasize issues surrounding local transport infrastructures as well as the right to decide (effectively national self-determination) rather than presenting independence as such as the necessary outcome. From 2009, the demand for a referendum emerged in a more palpable fashion through platforms promoting local 'consultations' on independence, taking advantage of provisions in Spain's referendum law that allowed private entities to organize them.

Catalonia 53

During this early embryonic phase of the process, there was already talk of the need to 'internationalize' the Catalan question, and the desire for Catalan statehood was posed in the context of Catalonia's European vocation. In July 2008, at the 15th congress of Convergència Democràtica de Catalunya (CDC), delegates overcame opposition from the leader of Convergència i Unió (CiU), Artur Mas, by voting for the objective of Catalonia becoming a 'free and sovereign nation in the Europe of the 21st century' as well as a 'state of our own', the latter being a more ambiguous formula thought likely by Mas to appeal to a wider Catalanist and regionalist spectrum of opinion. In March 2009, both CDC and Esquerra Republicana de Catalunya (ERC) backed a demonstration in Brussels, Belgium, by Catalan pro-independence civil society groups, attended by 10,000 activists, at which ERC's main candidate for the European elections, Oriol Junqueras, described the aim as being to 'internationalize the right to decide'. A banner read 'Catalonia is not Spain! Catalonia, the next state of Europe!' (*El País* 13 July 2008, 8 March 2009). The discourse of the independence movement was entirely positive both in relation to further European integration and the role that the EU might play in facilitating the desire of most Catalans to vote on their country's constitutional future. There was no attempt by the EU to discourage such hopes, largely because the main Catalan nationalist parties continued to be ambiguous on the issue of independence.

If before 2010 public agitation for a referendum went largely unremarked internationally, the protests over the Constitutional Court ruling, which attracted hundreds of thousands, possibly over a million people (Dowling 2013: 144), began to draw external attention and to indicate that something more than a passing dispute was unfolding in Catalonia. A poll commissioned by the Universitat Oberta de Catalunya in February had been the first to find a majority (50.3 per cent) ready to vote for independence in a hypothetical Catalan referendum, but far more (63 per cent) doubting that independence was possible (Nagel 2014: 344). To build and demonstrate truly massive support for independence on the streets, the Assemblea Nacional Catalana (ANC) went on to be formed in May 2011 as a civic association based on individual membership; cultural elites played a major role in this body which would mobilize vast numbers of independence supporters over the next few years, through activities held on Catalonia's national day, the *Diada* (Crameri 2014, 2015).

This phase saw growing grassroots demands for Catalan statehood, but nationalist parties were divided over the form that this should take and were uncertain about whether a complete break with Spain should be sought. Mas confirmed the centre-right orientation of his minority administration by negotiating support from the Partido Popular (PP) in the Catalan Parliament, in return for which he was prepared to bow to central government pressure to curb some of the Generalitat's international activity. During this period, Catalan Government demands were directed towards central government in Madrid and only a modest degree of lobbying took place externally. CiU's programme for the 2010 Catalan elections had emphasized the idea of negotiating a 'fiscal pact' with the Spanish Government, whereby Catalonia aimed to have its own tax agency and collect most of the taxes raised in the region, with a prospect sooner or later of being able to reduce the amount of revenue that it contributed to the Spanish treasury. That was the last Catalan parliamentary election of the decade to focus on economic rather than territorial issues (Gray 2020: 49–56; Barrio and Barberà 2011: 158). Meanwhile, ERC had campaigned on a pro-independence programme in 2010, but suffered a sharp reverse, dropping from third to fifth, penalized for having been in office during the early part of the recession and for deep internal divisions that had peaked around 2008. Pro-independence parties (a category that did not yet include CDC) saw their representation in the Catalan Parliament drop from 21 to 14 of the 135 seats (Dowling 2013: 158; see also Figure 3.1).

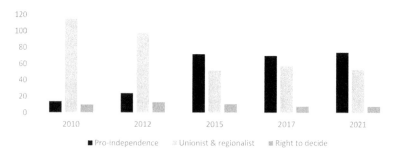

Figure 3.1 Territorial preferences in the Catalan Parliament, 2010–2021
Note: Numbers represent seats in the Catalan Parliament. The 'Right to decide' denotes parties that support a referendum but not necessarily Catalan independence. 'Pro-independence' includes ERC, JxSí, JxCat, the CUP and SI; 'Unionist & regionalist' includes PSC-PSOE, the PP, CiU, Cs and Vox; 'Right to decide' includes ICV, ECP and CSQP.

The secessionist turn in Catalan politics

CDC's outreach to other pro-sovereignty groups was a measure of its concern over an electoral trend that saw support for CiU waning while ERC, from 2011 under the presidency of Junqueras, regained its unity, attracted new support and began to show signs of becoming the leading pro-independence party. Mas attempted to reverse the trend by calling an early election to the Catalan Parliament in November 2012, after staging a rather theatrical trip to Madrid in September to meet the Spanish Prime Minister, Mariano Rajoy, knowing that the demand for a fiscal pact would be denied. The *Diada* earlier that month, organized by the ANC using the slogan 'Catalonia, next independent state in Europe', had taken mass mobilization to unprecedented levels, with some 8 per cent of the Catalan population of 7.5 million taking part. Although Mas warned that 'nobody is independent within the European Union' (*The Economist* 22 September 2012), these events marked the end of his attempts at negotiation with central government and the start of a more unilateral stage in which political sovereignty demands became central. Nonetheless, CiU's electoral programme was to remain ambiguous in demanding a 'state of our own' rather than independence. CiU saw its representation in the Catalan Parliament drop from 62 seats to 50, while that of ERC increased from 10 to 21 seats, thus becoming the second largest party in parliament. Solidaritat Catalana per la Independència (SI) lost the four seats it had won two years earlier (largely at the expense of ERC), but the Candidatura d'Unitat Popular (CUP) stood for the first time and won three seats. Although CiU lost 90,000 votes, pro-referendum parties now constituted 87 of the 135 seats in the Parliament, or 106 seats (including the Catalan Socialist Party) in the hypothetical case of an authorized referendum.

Cross-party united action among those advocating national self-determination was now seen as crucial to build on this balance of forces. The second Mas administration saw CiU working together with ERC in the creation of a Consell Assessor per a la Transició Nacional, recruited from among experts and academics to advise the Catalan Government on issues relating to self-determination and statehood for Catalonia. The Catalan campaign was also reinforced abroad through the opening of new official representational bodies. Developments here included the creation of Diplocat (an office tasked with organizing pro-sovereignty activity abroad, but which was shut down by the Constitutional Court in 2020) and the replacement of career diplomat Juan Prat with a political appointee as head of the

56 *Catalonia*

Catalan delegation in Brussels. The prime target of the diplomatic offensive was clearly the EU, notwithstanding a wider itinerary of visits including the USA. Catalan leaders had enjoyed exceptional levels of access to top EU officials in the past, but European concern over the rise of the independence movement led to the closing of such avenues after 2011. Nonetheless, the Spanish Government soon felt the need to lobby hard for international support over Catalonia, its case against a referendum being that, constitutionally, sovereignty was vested in the people of Spain and thus Catalonia had no rights in the matter.

During this phase, Mas initially intended to consult Catalans simply on whether they wished Catalonia to become a new state of the EU, rather than seek a mandate to declare independence, but this perspective became increasingly problematic. Alarmed by developments in Catalonia, which included a parliamentary declaration of sovereignty in 2013, and concerned about the refusal (or incapacity) of Mariano Rajoy's Government to negotiate with its Catalan counterpart, EU leaders (including European Commission President José Manuel Durão Barroso), who hitherto had largely avoided commenting on the 'internal affairs' of Spain, began to warn that a new Catalan state would start its life outside the EU and would need support for accession from all the existing member states, including Spain (on the Prodi doctrine, see Chapter 1 in this volume). Mas himself now accepted that an independent Catalonia would find itself temporarily out of the EU, trusting that the Scottish referendum would help its prospects. The tone, also reflected in a Consell Assessor report on the implications of independence for European membership, remained optimistic, implying some form of benign deal with the EU to see Catalonia through a transition period (Generalitat de Catalunya 2014); meanwhile, warnings from some European leaders that Catalonia would find itself at the back of the queue formed by existing accession states were disbelieved, given that Catalonia formed part of the EU.

Rajoy's policy on Catalonia was marked not only by intransigence but also by recentralizing measures that were political and cultural as well as economic. In common with other Spanish debt-laden regions, Catalonia was forced to adjust its budget drastically in return for central financial support while it also found itself suffering somewhat disproportionately from cuts in Spanish investment during the recession. Politically driven recentralization efforts by the PP were seen in judicial action to counter Catalan moves to develop a fully fledged diplomatic service, a new Spanish External Action Law controlling external activity by the autonomous communities, and the so-called

Catalonia 57

Wert Law designed in part to weaken the status of Catalan as the language of teaching delivery in schools.

The lack of a constructive political response from Madrid helped to polarize the perception of options in Catalonia, and in September 2013 an even bigger *Diada* mobilization took place, during which 1.6 million Catalans created a 400-km 'human chain' extending from north to south of the country that was inspired by the 'Baltic Way' of 1989 in Estonia, Latvia and Lithuania. Catalan sovereignty activists had been encouraged by the Edinburgh Agreement of 2012 and subsequent referendum process in Scotland (see Chapter 4 in this volume). Under strong pressure from civil society activism demanding that independence itself be voted on, Mas eventually went ahead with a non-binding consultation in November 2014, posing two questions, 'Do you want Catalonia to become a state?' and, if so, 'Do you want this state to be independent?' Boycotted by the unionist parties on the right and by the Partit dels Socialistes de Catalunya (PSC) leadership for being unconstitutional, the significance of this event was far from clear. The Generalitat announced that 2.3 million people had voted but did not give a percentage for turnout (which estimates suggested was between 37–42 per cent); 80.8 per cent of the participants had voted 'yes' and 'yes', and 10.1 per cent 'yes' and 'no' (*La Vanguardia* 10 November 2014). The vote took place in defiance of a Constitutional Court ban, following an appeal against it by the Spanish Government. Later, Mas and members of his Government went on trial for holding an illegal vote in defiance of Spanish court rulings; subsequently, they were banned from public office and fined.

While expressing the hope that Catalonia would become a new state of the EU, Mas sought to avoid the spectre of separation and its evident potential to alienate cautious voters and business sectors. His message was that he stood for 'more Catalonia' and 'more Europe' but not 'less Spain', with which he wanted an ongoing relationship (*El País* 23 September 2013). At this time the debate was much more about the 'right to decide' than the impact of a hypothetical independence.

In interviews and statements given between 2012 and 2015, Mas's estimations of whether a new Catalan state would be able to remain in the EU via an internal enlargement varied: at times he maintained that, as the seventh largest economy in the EU and a net contributor, the Union itself (and even Spain) had an interest in Catalonia remaining in the bloc, while on other occasions he claimed that there would be a relatively short accession process since it already met the requisites of membership. During a transatlantic visit in April 2015,

58 *Catalonia*

notwithstanding Catalonia's high level of indebtedness, he presented an optimistic vision of it becoming for a future united states of Europe what Massachusetts was to the USA.

The pursuit of Catalan independence and the launch of the *Procés*

Although the Catalan push for a referendum had begun, independence had yet to be placed firmly on the political agenda. This was done during the next phase (2015–2017) known in Catalonia as the *Procés*, commencing with another regional election in which independence forces obtained a mandate to proceed unilaterally, if necessary. It culminated in the referendum of October 2017 and the Spanish response. In itself, the Catalan 2015 election was not as convincing a victory for the independence parties as many of their leaders had hoped (see Figure 3.1). Although CDC and ERC joined forces, together with smaller parties and personalities from the ANC and Òmnium Cultural, to present a common list called Junts pel Sí (JxSí) and came close to winning an absolute majority of the seats, its 39.6 per cent share of the vote, garnering it 62 seats, meant that it needed to negotiate with the radical CUP (8.2 per cent, 10 seats) to secure an effective majority.

Riding the crest of a wave, the anti-capitalists held the balance of power and were able to secure concessions in social policy and a change of government leader in return for supporting the creation of a pro-independence government. The CUP vetoed a further administration led by Mas, whom they opposed for his neoliberal policies and vacillating pursuit of sovereignty while in office; in his stead the new President of the Generalitat was the mayor of Girona, Carles Puigdemont, who had long advocated independence within CDC (Puigdemont interview 2013). More of a centrist in left-right terms, his investiture as President was crucial to establishing collaboration between JxSí and the CUP and ensuring that independence became the only game in town for the new administration, with policy initiatives losing priority.

This period witnessed further efforts to reinforce the external diplomatic campaign by the Generalitat through the creation of a new department headed by Raül Romeva, although this was immediately suspended by Spain's Constitutional Court. Puigdemont himself tried to present the plans for a referendum to international leaders, not least in Brussels and the USA, but he was not received at the highest EU levels, as his predecessors had been before the possibility of independence appeared on the horizon. In January 2016, he recognized

Catalonia 59

that the parliamentary basis for a unilateral declaration of independence was still not present, yet still proposed to hold a referendum and presented this as a democratic assertion of rights rather than an expression of identity-based nationalism. The draft law for Catalonia's secession from Spain in the event of a 'yes' vote in the referendum, eventually scheduled for 1 October 2017, was itself deeply controversial within the Catalan Parliament, where a large minority of deputies objected to the procedures used to organize a referendum in defiance of Spanish court rulings on their illegality and the illegality of the referendum itself. The great contrast with the Scottish referendum would be the boycott of the event by unionists and indeed by some Catalans who wanted a referendum but were opposed to the way it was brought about. Hence the interest in the outcome of the Catalan referendum lay in the turnout (43 per cent) and the number of people voting 'yes' (two million, 92 per cent of those voting) to the question 'Do you want Catalonia to become an independent state in the form of a republic?'

Although no thresholds had been set for the outcome to be deemed valid by the Catalan Government, this result gave pause for thought even to Puigdemont, who initially postponed a parliamentary Unilateral Declaration of Independence in the hope that European leaders would discreetly try to persuade Rajoy to negotiate. Despite the fragility of the outcome as a mandate for secession, what was encouraging to the independence movement was that so many Catalans had taken part despite judicial bans and a massive Spanish police operation designed to prevent voting, leading to ugly events in which policemen charged and beat peaceful civilians. Hundreds of people were injured in scenes of repression that shocked television viewers, not least in other EU countries. What many saw as an overreaction to the referendum by the Rajoy Government persuaded some Catalan doubters in the end to cast 'yes' votes, while for many international spectators it tended to legitimize the voting. For them, it was the police violence rather than constitutional improprieties by the pro-independence parties that became the predominant image of the day's events.

Further concern about Spain's handling of the challenge was expressed towards the end of October when the Catalan Parliament finally voted to declare independence and the central authorities responded by invoking Article 155 of the Spanish Constitution, thereby dissolving the Parliament and suspending Catalonia's autonomy prior to announcing a regional election in December. Members of the deposed Puigdemont Government, together with other

60 *Catalonia*

promotors of the referendum, were then imprisoned, pending trial, or fled abroad. Although widely applauded in many parts of Spain, the decision to imprison pro-independence leaders encountered a more questioning attitude abroad. While EU leaders expressed the view that the Spanish Government had acted constitutionally, human rights groups, part of the media and other sections of European civil society began to criticize Madrid's actions. Moreover, the decision by Puigdemont and other government members to go into exile in Brussels helped the independence movement to present the Catalan conflict to a wider audience as it resisted Spanish attempts at extradition through European courts, created unofficial new representative bodies that would meet outside of Spain, staged further demonstrations abroad and prepared for the next round of elections to the European Parliament.

Puigdemont, in contrast to both his immediate predecessor and especially to Pujol earlier, initially adopted a more low-key discourse on Europe, although he travelled abroad quite extensively to solicit support for the referendum plans. Despite a series of rebuffs from European leaders, he told fellow Catalans that, whereas he had found signs of European concern about Spanish policy, he believed that the EU would adopt a pragmatic response in the event of Catalan independence. He cited the warm reception in Brussels of the First Minister of Scotland, Nicola Sturgeon, in the wake of the Brexit referendum (see Chapter 4 in this volume) as evidence that the EU discourse on Scotland and Catalonia was changing and he publicly continued to invest hope in the Union, while acknowledging that its response to some developments, such as the refugee crisis, was regrettably slow (*El Diario.es* 25 June 2016; *El Periódico de Catalunya* 30 June 2016).

By attempting to prevent the referendum and punish those held responsible for it, the Spanish authorities contributed to polarization in Catalonia, where support for independence parties held up well when the December election was held, as they benefited from a sharpened sense of injustice and an emotional desire to show solidarity with the prisoners. Spanish intransigence ensured that the larger of these parties would continue to work together, although on this occasion ERC presented its own lists, competing with a new platform called JxCat. While this included a CDC successor party, the Partit Demòcrata Europeu Català (PDeCAT), Puigdemont used his own political authority to exert the main influence on the composition of its lists. Polarization was seen in the victory of the unionist Ciudadanos (Cs) party, up from 11 to 36 seats, while JxCat (21.7 per cent, 31seats) and ERC (21.4 per cent, 26 seats) retained their coalition

Catalonia 61

potential and the CUP (4.5 per cent, four seats) lost support to JxCat. Eventually, with Cs unable to assemble a majority in Parliament, independent Puigdemont supporter Quim Torra came to head a JxCat-ERC minority coalition between 2018–2020, a period that also saw growing division and fragmentation within the ranks of the pro-independence forces.

Diverging strategies among Catalan pro-independence forces

The final phase depicted here lasted from 2017 to 2021. During this period, Torra's efforts to maintain the momentum of the independence process came up against further judicial injunctions and bans (which eventually led to his being debarred from office by the Spanish Supreme Court in 2020), a decline in popular mobilization and a de facto abandonment of unilateralism by ERC. The latter had reached the conclusion that the independence movement required a substantially larger basis of support before it could achieve its ambitions: at least one-half of Catalan voters would need to support it on an ongoing basis; further fluctuation within the 40 per cent to 50 per cent range would not suffice (see Chapter 1 in this volume). To build support, ERC adopted more pragmatic attitudes while seeking in the short term to exert influence within the Spanish political system. Pragmatism was seen in its readiness to support the budgets of the second city administration headed by Ada Colau in Barcelona, formed by Barcelona en Comú and the Socialists, after it had outpolled both individually in the municipal elections of 2019, and in its readiness to help Pedro Sánchez to become Prime Minister of a PSOE-Unidas Podemos (UP) coalition Government in January 2020 by abstaining in the investiture vote. ERC responded positively to Sánchez's offer of dialogue with the Catalan Government and saw the Spanish left as a preferable government interlocutor to a potential alternative coalition based on collaboration between the PP, Cs and Vox, a far-right party founded in 2013. Its pragmatism was accentuated during 2020, as the coronavirus (COVID-19) pandemic hit Catalonia particularly severely: coping with a public health crisis and prioritizing the need to give urgent attention to its social and economic sequels partially overshadowed the territorial issue and brought important instances of constructive cooperation between ERC and the Sánchez Government in Madrid. The disunity of the pro-independence parties over how to behave there was seen in December when pro-Puigdemont Junts deputies opposed the Government's new budget in the Congress of Deputies while ERC (decisively) voted for it, as did

62 Catalonia

the smaller PDeCAT, which earlier had rejected Puigdemont's effort to reunify various former CiU sectors through establishing JxCat as a political party.

With ERC and JxCat now almost level in opinion polls, rivalry was especially evident as the pro-independence parties prepared for another early Catalan election in February 2021. Whichever of these parties emerged ahead of the other would attempt to impress their strategic stamp on the next government of Catalonia. The winner was the Socialist Party (PSC-PSOE), which stole a march on its rivals by adopting as its candidate Minister of Health Salvador Illa, well known for managing Spain's response to the pandemic. However, despite leading with 23 per cent of the vote and doubling their representation in parliament, the Socialists, with 33 seats, were not able to form a coalition. Thus, as in 2015, an overall majority was within the grasp of the independence parties if they could agree to act together (see Figure 3.1). ERC had won 21 per cent of the vote (33 seats), JxCat 20 percent (32 seats) and the CUP 6.6 per cent (9 seats), while the PDeCAT on 2.72 per cent failed to gain representation. For the first time, pro-independence parties had won just over 50 per cent of the vote, yet the appearance of a stronger mandate was flawed by a big drop in turn-out. With the election taking place during the pandemic, participation fell by almost 28 per cent, to 51.3 per cent.

This was the phase in which Catalan pro-independence leaders began to acquire a higher profile in relation to EU institutions. Although the larger parties did have Members of the European Parliament (MEPs) who had been elected in previous elections, in 2019 the opportunity afforded by EP elections was used more strategically to internationalize the Catalan conflict. ERC's list was headed by the imprisoned Junqueras (prevented by the Spanish authorities from taking up his seat) while JxCat successfully presented Puigdemont and Antoni Comín, another former member of the Catalan Government whose extradition was sought by Spain. Although EP President Antonio Tajani prevented the latter duo from being issued with passes along with the other newly elected MEPs, an appeal by Junqueras led the Court of Justice of the European Union (CJEU) to rule in December 2019 that he had parliamentary immunity from the moment of his election, regardless of Spanish formalities for the naming of its MEPs. This did not enable Junqueras to leave prison to take up his seat, but did allow Puigdemont, Comín and – following post-Brexit seat reallocations – Clara Ponsatí to take up theirs. Moves by Spanish unionists to have this reversed resulted in March 2021 in these MEPs having their immunity lifted by the EP, albeit with significant divisions in the progressive and liberal groups (the vote in Puigdemont's case being 400–248 with 45 abstentions). The PSOE voted for, UP against.

Both the imprisonment of *Procés* leaders prior to their trial in 2019 and the eventual sentencing of nine of the 12 accused to terms of incarceration ranging from nine to 13 years on charges of sedition, and in some cases misuse of public funds, gave the independence movement a basis for complaints and legal action over human rights violations. The human rights organization, Amnesty International, found that, while the trial by the Supreme Court had conformed with international law, the crime of sedition had been interpreted too widely and that the Presidents of the ANC and Òmnium Cultural should not have been imprisoned for 'entirely peaceful' acts (Amnesty International 2019).

Spanish extradition efforts resumed following the lifting of the MEPs' immunity, yet there were several morale-raising triumphs for the independence parties in this period: court rulings against Spanish extradition requests in Belgium, Switzerland, the UK and Germany, variously based on the lack of equivalents to the Spanish crime of 'rebellion' (cited in extradition documents), the way in which Spain's Supreme Court interpreted 'sedition', the lack of competence of that court (as opposed to a Catalan court) to judge cases and the risk of defendants' rights being violated in respect of the presumption of innocence if they were extradited to Spain; and a sympathetic resolution approved by the Parliamentary Assembly of the Council of Europe in June 2021, which upset Spanish representatives by placing Spain's response to the Catalan challenge in the same context as authoritarian Turkey's treatment of Kurdish secessionists (*El País* 24 June 2021). When released following partial pardons by the Sánchez Government in the same month, the nine imprisoned leaders of the independence movement attributed this event to ongoing electoral victories, judicial successes in Europe and popular mobilization.

By 2021, Spanish responses to the Catalan independence challenge still counted with considerable European and international endorsement, but the events of October 2017 and its aftermath had led to a turn in the tide, if not a sea change, in external responses to the ongoing contest between independence supporters and Spanish unionists. There was now much wider recognition that a political problem existed and had been exacerbated by the way the Spanish authorities had responded to it, particularly under Rajoy. Moreover, international organizations and foreign courts were now involved in the matter much more than some five to ten years earlier.

64   *Catalonia*

Internationalization of the Catalan question had become at least a partial reality.

The changing discourse on Europe among Catalan pro-independence forces

Under the impact of the events of October 2017, there was a sharp shift in Puigdemont's discourse on the EU, particularly in reaction to the lack of concern expressed by European leaders over the Spanish clampdown. 'Are they going to continue supporting Rajoy in this *coup d'état* and restriction of freedom?' he asked. 'Is that the Europe they want? One that sends a government to prison?' Puigdemont's invective was principally directed against 'the clan of the 155', that is, the Spanish parties that had voted for the suspension of Catalan autonomy, but in a very personal way he asked 'Mr Juncker, Mr Tajani, why have you not reacted against the abuses [committed by] a failed democracy' (*El País* 8 November 2017). In interviews, he now regularly expressed disappointment at the EU response, not over independence itself but rather with reference to fundamental European values having been violated without the Union speaking out over 'police brutality' or 'political repression' (*El País* 28 September 2018). Further criticisms of EP President Antonio Tajani for facilitating 'anti-democratic regression' in Europe followed the latter's ban on Puigdemont addressing a meeting in the Parliament in February 2019 and then in May when Tajani intervened to stop the handover of provisional passes to Spanish MEPs, in order to prevent Puigdemont and Comín from gaining admission. When the pro-independence MEPs were finally permitted to take up their seats in January 2020, Puigdemont declared that the EU could no longer look the other way, since the question of Catalonia had come to have an impact on its constitutional basis and was now the subject of European court deliberations. He criticized the nature of the EU when appearing in the documentary, *Two Catalonias* (2018), directed by Álvaro Longoria and Gerardo Olivares, contending that the EU had made the mistake of trying to 'homogenize' the nature of its members; it would have been better to build on the cultural richness emanating from different 'historic peoples' of Europe.

Notwithstanding their strategic differences, an examination of election programmes and party conference documents shows a substantial ongoing consensus between ERC and JxCat on European issues. The desire to see Catalan become an official language of the EU had been a major emphasis of CiU and ERC documents for the 2011 general

Catalonia 65

election, with ERC calling moreover for greater political integration and democratization of the EU. By the time of the European elections of 2014, the Catalan referendum push was very much in evidence, particularly in the ERC programme, which urged the EU to recognize the 'right to decide' as a fundamental right and to try to persuade Spain of this view. The electoral programme presented by JxSí one year later emphasized that an independent Catalonia would seek 'continuity' in the EU and remain part of the Eurozone (JxSí 2015: 51).

However, there was some qualification of the pro-European positions adopted by the main parties of government following the disappointing official silence of the EU in the wake of the events of 2017. JxCat's programme in December stated: 'We are and we feel European. But we want to live in a different Europe, with fully democratic institutions and commitments to its values', while stressing too that it wanted to see the emergence of a truly federal Europe (JxCat 2017: 7–8). ERC's programme for the general election in April 2019 (the first of two in that year) similarly advocated a 'Catalan republic in a federal Europe', with the EU ceasing to be a 'club of states' (ERC 2019a: 23). JxCat's programme for the following Catalan election was considerably more detailed on European matters, advocating a federal Europe based on increased qualified majority voting, direct election of the President of the Commission, transnational lists in EP elections, EP powers of legislative initiative, and direct involvement of regions and stateless nations in decision-making. It called for the EU to make legal provision for internal enlargement and proposed a European Clarity Law, establishing procedures and stipulating majorities for the creation of new states within the EU. Both JxCat and ERC remained very much open to fiscal union and Junts also backed defence integration, subject to the EU's structure being democratized (JxCat 2021; ERC 2021).

The partial successes achieved by the Catalan independence forces in Europe following the 2017 events helped to neutralize the temptation of Euroscepticism that disappointments over elite EU behaviour might otherwise have engendered, although independence leaders expressed concern that public support for Europe might eventually be undermined if EU policy remained unchanged in relation to the question of Catalonia (interviews CAT 2; CAT 3). Evidence of ongoing underlying positivity on Europe was seen too in the political resolutions passed at party congresses. ERC's political resolution passed in November 2019 did not refer specifically to Europe as such, but implied continuity with earlier positions when stating that it would continue to work with the Greens as part of the European Free

66 Catalonia

Alliance. The resolution had a more conciliatory tone, claiming that it was now possible for pro-independence forces to win more than 50 per cent of the vote in Catalan elections and held repeated instances of this to be a necessary although insufficient condition for creating a republic. ERC believed that it remained impossible to negotiate with Spain on a self-determination referendum, yet nevertheless stated that it would work towards this goal by defending Catalonia's institutions, engaging in dialogue with central government, maintaining constant mobilization and building international support. While the party did not rule out a unilateral path to another referendum as one of three possible courses of action, it expressed a clear preference for a negotiated path, which might eventually be possible if both national and international support grew (ERC 2019b).

In contrast, the programme adopted by JxCat in October 2020 made direct reference to a potential EU role in resolving the conflict and stuck to the more unilateralist strategy of civil disobedience and 'peaceful, intelligent confrontation' with the Spanish state. Like ERC, however, JxCat recognized that the independence forces would need an overall majority in the next Catalan election to progress. Armed with a firmer electoral mandate than they had obtained in 2015 and 2017, they could then ask the EU to mediate and to persuade the Spanish Government to authorize a referendum. The political resolution echoed Puigdemont's own recognition that there was work still to do to convince the EU that the Catalan movement was not a case of 'identity-based nationalism' but rather was about building 'a more democratic and just society' (JxCat 2020). 'We are not going to lose our patience', he stated in a final message to the online congress.

JxCat's position was now making support for some aspects of European integration conditional, implying that it might not remain positive unless democratization took place and the Union took steps to uphold its fundamental values. 'Europeanism', together with feminism, ecologism and democratic radicalism (*la radicalitat democràtica*) were proclaimed as four transversal social currents that would allow Catalonia to progress, but the espoused Catalan republic was now depicted 'in the context of a European Union that recovers its founding values, that makes a clear defence of human and fundamental rights and advances towards more integration and democratization. The future of Europe is not the Europe of States but the Europe of the citizenry' (JxCAT 2020). Rather than continuing with the negative theme of disappointment, participants at the JxCat congress defined themselves as '*euroexigents*', demanding the restoration of traditional European ideals and not merely a more sympathetic understanding of the Catalan situation. The EU was still described as an opportunity for Catalonia, while on the other hand, the latter was presented as an opportunity for the Union to base itself on smaller national states and thereby promote greater democracy and diversity (JxCat 2020).

The evidence from party congresses shows the growing differences between ERC and JxCat at this time to be most explicitly to do with their attitudes towards Spain: the extent to which dialogue might be beneficial to the independence movement and whether confrontation should continue. ERC's political resolution even contained a short section on 'democratic fraternity with the peoples of Spain', reflecting its readiness to work with left-wing forces in other parts of the country. Elite interviews also indicate that the two parties continued to have much in common over Europe, regardless of the amount of attention it received in congress resolutions. During interviews conducted in 2019 representatives of both JxCat and ERC expressed great disappointment with EU responses to events in Catalonia, and this was seen as an alarming failure to defend fundamental values, yet without this translating into anti-EU postures. Rather, the emphasis was on promoting reforms of the EU and taking every opportunity to place the principles of national self-determination and defence of its citizens more firmly among the values the Union should uphold (interviews CAT 1; CAT 2; CAT 3; CAT 4; CAT 5; CAT 6).

Ongoing commitment to the EU was evident too in a white paper produced by the Generalitat during the JxCat-ERC coalition government headed by Torra in 2018–2020, the *Pla Europa*, which drew upon civil society consultations. A response to the European Commission's own white paper on the Future of Europe (European Commission 2017) and ensuing reflection papers, it demonstrated the continuing desire of the Catalan Government to take part in European debates over a wide range of issues, while specific Catalan goals were highlighted in an introduction by Alfred Bosch, in which he referred to a need to find ways of governing that might 'foster the increased presence and impact of stateless nations, regions, cities and cross border macro regions' in an EU that he hoped would become 'a common space that stands up for linguistic diversity, economic and territorial cohesion and participatory democracy' (Generalitat de Catalunya 2019). Notwithstanding the positive tone, this text seemed to indicate that the coalition's desire to change the status quo was now almost as radical in relation to Europe as it was with respect to Spain: a position that did not auger well for Catalan hopes to see the EU play an even-handed mediation role any time soon.

68 Catalonia

Much more negative, meanwhile, was the position of the CUP, whose support would once again be necessary for the creation of a pro-independence government following the Catalan elections scheduled to take place in March 2021. The anti-capitalists went into this election with an uncompromising programme in which they refused to recognize an EU whose *raison d'être* was to 'guarantee the privileges of capital' and their notion of 'internationalization' of the Catalan conflict was simply to collaborate with other radical left-wing organizations in Europe (CUP 2021: 104, 122).

Catalan public opinion and party elite views on Europe

A crucial point of reference for the deployment of 'Europe' as an instrument of opposing sides in the Catalan conflict was the evolution of public opinion. Studies of this at the level of autonomous communities have always been limited by the scarcity of data compared to that available at the state level, yet there are enough on Catalonia to offer some pointers, indicating why EU warnings about negative effects of secession have had less impact than Union and member state leaders may have expected, namely not enough of an impact to deter political actors from pursuing the objective of self-determination. While arguing that EU support for its member state helped to legitimize the Spanish response to the Catalan challenge, Aumaitre (2017) cites CEO survey data for 2013–2017 showing that, whereas levels of public trust in the EU in Catalonia previously had not varied in accordance with the positions held by people in the disagreement over the autonomous community's relationship to Spain, this period did see a diminution of trust among independence supporters and those who identified themselves as 'only Catalan' (that is, not also Spanish) in 2016 and more strikingly in 2017, while in contrast the level of trust did increase among those who believed that Catalonia should remain part of Spain and those who felt to some degree Spanish (see Figure 3.2). Whereas at the start of the sequence it was only CUP voters that indicated a lack of trust in the EU, this became more widespread among voters for pro-independence parties. Although the breakup of CiU and the post-CDC division that gave rise to the PDeCAT and JxCat complicate the analysis of such data in relation to voting behaviour, there was certainly a significant drop in trust of the EU among PDeCAT voters, who showed almost as much detachment from the EU as CUP and ERC voters by the end of 2017 (Aumaitre 2017).

This seems to imply at least the possibility of a rising current of Euroscepticism in Catalonia if EU opposition to self-determination by

Catalonia 69

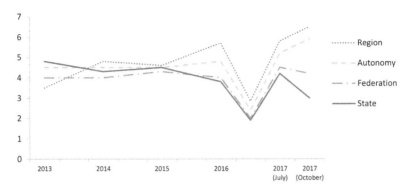

Figure 3.2 Trust in the EU by territorial preference in Catalonia, 2013–2017
Note: Trust in the EU measured on a scale of 0 (low) to 10 (high). 'Region' denotes that the respondent wants to reduce Catalonia's autonomy; 'autonomy' denotes a preference for the status quo; 'federation' denotes a preference for constitutional reforms to make Spain a federal state; 'state' denotes a preference for Catalan independence.
Source: Aumaitre (2017).

Catalans were to persist. What seems clear, however, is that public concern about whether an independent Catalonia would be able to remain part of the EU, more or less without interruption, proved to be much less of a deterrent in persuading Catalans to retreat from the ambition of statehood than the leaders of EU institutions may have expected. In a web-based survey looking comparatively at how prospects of EU membership have influenced support for secession in Catalonia and Scotland, Muro and Vlaskamp found similarly that 'the prospects of EU membership had only a limited effect on the creation of a sovereign state' and that, to the extent that there was an impact, it was strongly mediated by the survey participant's 'previous degree of nationalism and their attitudes towards the EU' (2016: 1115). Only citizens with moderate nationalist beliefs and pro-European attitudes were influenced. Moreover, the opponents of the Catalan pro-sovereignty movement had made so many threats about the consequences for EU membership that, before the battle reached a climax in 2017, Catalans had already incorporated them into their political calculations. The most pro-EU participants in the survey were less likely to vote for independence in the referendum, while those who already distrusted the EU were not affected by talk of negative consequences (ibid.: 1130–1131). For most Catalans in the pro-independence camp, the determination to secede from Spain seemed to override whatever calculations they made about future membership of the EU. While it

70 *Catalonia*

may certainly have been a factor affecting their chances of securing an overall voting majority, the widespread assumption was that, sooner or later, the new Catalonia would form part of the EU.

The evolution of public opinion left pro-independence elites under little pressure to choose between Europe and the pursuit of statehood. During the preparatory years of the *Procés*, political and civil society leaders advocating Catalan independence were invariably positive when asked about their expectations of the EU, notwithstanding warnings from the European Commission that an independent Catalonia would need to apply for EU membership as a 'third country', from the outside. Interviewees from CDC (Lluís Corominas, Santi Vila), UDC (Núria de Gispert), ERC (Alfred Bosch, Oriol Amorós as well as former PSC politician Ernest Maragall who would eventually join this party) and the ANC (Carme Forcadell), questioned in 2013–2014, all argued that the EU's recent evolution had left it largely a club of member states, but used that as a basis for justifying Catalonia's desire for statehood so that it could play a bigger role and exert its influence in Europe, rather than viewing this as an EU characteristic that might justify Catalan Euroscepticism.

The positivity of responses was associated in any case with an underlying historical attachment to Europe, the fundamental values espoused by the EU and the fact that it was Spain that was perceived as the major problem for Catalonia. The philologist Forcadell, commenting that Catalan was more widely spoken than some official languages of the EU, attributed this fact to Spain's supposed failure to support Catalan, rather than blaming the Union. Amorós, who described himself as a social democrat, said: 'The EU is a club of member states, but it is a democratic club. For us, Europe is democracy, it is peace and modernization. We want to be Swedish!' (Amorós interview 2014). Most respondents insisted that Catalonia was more pro-EU than the rest of Spain, recent lower participation in European parliamentary elections being attributed by de Gispert to the dominance within the EP of the two big Socialist and Popular blocs. Although the claims have a historical basis, there was some exaggeration here. Analysing opinion poll data from 1973–2015, Cetrà and Liñeira (2018) found that Catalonia showed very similar levels of trust in EC/EU institutions to the rest of Spain (although the Basque Country less so).

There was also a widely held view among our interviewees that the Catalan pro-referendum forces would not have been able to get as far as they had were it not for the very existence of the EU acting as a restraint upon the counter-measures available to the Spanish state.

Catalonia 71

The only dissenting position on Europe was that of the CUP, which opposed the EU as representing 'the Europe of capital' and a 'threat to the popular classes'; yet although it proposed leaving the Eurozone and the Union itself, it generally muted its opposition to the EU in deference to mainstream public opinion and because it wanted to avoid bringing a divisive issue into the independence movement (*El Mundo* 13 September 2015; CUP 2021; Arrufat interview 2014). Public opinion at this time remained so strongly Europhile that one former SI MP spoke of 'an unnaturally big prejudice in favour of Europe' among Catalan independence supporters, who continued to look upon Europe as a kind of saviour (Strubell interview 2014).

Whether the Catalan process would entail a Catalan departure from the EU, and if so for how long and with what transitional arrangements, were major focuses in political debates on the question of independence. Early on, the main pro-independence parties had high hopes of an internal enlargement of the EU proving possible. In October 2012, a statement by the then Vice-President of the European Commission responsible for justice issues, Viviane Reding, about international law not specifying that a secessionist state would need to leave the EU, was latched onto jubilantly by independence supporters, only for its effect to be neutralized by other statements emanating from the Commission to the effect that international law only stated how a new state should be treated by the international community and that the call for a Catalan right to decide was a matter for Spain to resolve through dialogue between its government and Catalonia (*El País* 12 October 2012). For independence activists, this by no means resolved the issue, for the negative warnings at this time came largely from the Commission and occasionally the European Parliament, whereas ultimately it would be the European Council that would need to decide the matter, in the event of independence being declared and Catalonia approaching the EU to discuss membership. In the absence of a direct precedent, there was some possibility, as mooted by certain academics, that the future circumstances might lead the Union to decide that it was a matter of an existing member state being dissolved, rather than a question of secession (Duerr 2015: 152). Looking to the intergovernmental dimension of the EU, independence advocates could point to some signs of sympathy, especially in the smaller member states, although initial support for a Catalan referendum from the Prime Ministers of Lithuania and Estonia was withdrawn following protests from the Spanish Ministry of Foreign Affairs in September 2013.

Arguments used by independence politicians to reassure Catalans that self-determination would not ultimately prove disruptive to

72 *Catalonia*

membership of the EU were largely based on the value of Catalonia to the EU, which would ensure that even if there was an accession period to be traversed, it would be accompanied by transitional arrangements that would effectively maintain much of the status quo. They included the following claims, not all of them congruent:

- Catalonia already met the conditions for EU membership, so there would be no need for a potentially long accession process involving an alignment of norms and practices.
- Technically, leaving the EU is a long process, during which realistic negotiations could take place on Catalan membership.
- Catalans are European citizens; it would be harsh and indeed improbable for the EU to 'expel' them.
- The EU would not wish to lose 7.5 million consumers and a net contributor to the budget.
- Nor, if it came to separation, would the EU, multinational companies or Spain itself benefit from having an 'outsider' located between the heart of Europe and the Iberian member states.

These arguments were formidable enough to help to sustain the unity of the pro-independence camp and permit its growth in the early years of the process, but they ignored the damage that separation itself might do to Catalan-Spanish relations and the potential for it to facilitate an advance by the far right and fuel illiberal sentiments that would ignore the logic of mutual interest. The contention that the EU would not be prepared to lose Catalonia was contested by Spanish economist Ángel de la Fuente, who maintained that several member states were likely to oppose an EU application by Catalonia, which in any case represented just 1.44 per cent of the EU's population and 1.5 per cent of its gross domestic product in 2012 (*El País* 15 October 2013).

Catalan governmental assumptions were not based simply on a mix of rational calculation and wishful thinking, but also on feedback derived from contact between independence leaders and European and other international interlocutors. From various consultations at the level of diplomats and senior officials in the EU, those working for a 'right to decide' began to realize early on that member states would not be moved by the massive demonstrations coordinated by the ANC and that the EU would not be persuaded to adopt a position on Catalonia until after there had been a popular vote on its future. The EU would not act against a member state, but if relations with the Spanish state reached a crisis point, then member states might shift position

Catalonia 73

(Bosch interview 2013). In the event, member states did not start to move on the issue in 2017, yet this did not bring a change of international perspective in the strategic thinking of the independence movement. In the aftermath of the events of the October referendum, Europe continued to loom just as large in Catalan deliberations. Interviewed in 2019, an official in the Generalitat maintained that the EU still had a role to play in the Catalan conflict (interview CAT 1). While some EU officials, not least Jean-Claude Juncker, had been particularly hostile to the referendum process, the interviewee hoped that the new series of EU leaders taking office in December might play a more discrete, constructive role in the future. Another interviewee argued that without the EU context, the Spanish Government would have brought in the military to prevent the October referendum (interview CAT 4). This participant was doubtful about the EU as a potential mediator in the Catalan conflict but saw the possibility that another member state might prove helpful (ibid.). Another official in the Generalitat argued that the way in which the Rajoy Government had dealt with the Catalan challenge had opened up new opportunities for Europe to play a more even-handed role (interview CAT 2). By establishing the case that Spain had used repression against the independence movement, the latter would be in a stronger position to counter the EU argument that Catalonia was an internal matter for Spain. While territorial integrity and devolution were certainly member state prerogatives under the EU treaties, fundamental values and human rights were clearly European and international matters (ibid.). Another interviewee acknowledged disappointment at the EU role thus far but held that it would not benefit this person's political party to adopt a Eurosceptic position (interview CAT 5). If Spain continued to prove unable to find a solution to the Catalan question, the EU would become more involved, applying pressure for realistic solutions. However, several interviewees independently of one another said that ultimately there was a need to find the solution 'ourselves', with Spain (interviews CAT 1; CAT 4; CAT 5).

The tone of thinking within the main parties thus remained positive despite the reverse experienced in 2017, partly because the independence movement had gone some way towards transforming defeat into victory, helped by what many outside observers believed to have been an overreaction by Spain. The fact that courts in various European countries refused to extradite Catalan leaders who had taken up residence abroad demonstrated that part of the international community either did not recognize the crimes of rebellion and sedition of which independence leaders were accused, or had doubts about whether the

74 *Catalonia*

accused would receive a fair trial and proportional sentence in Spain, or alternatively objected to Spanish actions on procedural grounds. Equally, the CJEU ruling in the Junqueras case provided a pretext for Puigdemont and two former members of his former Government, who had also left Spain, to occupy seats in the EP, although efforts to remove their immunity continued. There they were able to draw upon additional resources and Puigdemont himself became a more prominent focal point for the independence movement. An EU-Catalonia Platform for Dialogue had already been established there and in April 2018 some 44 MEPs from 15 EU member states had signed its manifesto calling for dialogue in Catalonia, the release of the nine separatist leaders from prison, non-extradition by European countries of the exiles on the grounds that they would not get a fair trial in Spain, and for EU institutions to mediate to find a political solution. Placing this in context, the signatories did not greatly exceed the number of 30 MEPs who were members of the platform (*El País* 12 April 2018).

Frans Timmermans, as Commissioner for the Charter of Fundamental Rights, declared in February 2019 that the European Commission had no criticisms of the state of law, democracy or human rights in Spain. On the other hand, the EU's attitude towards the accession of an eventual independent Scotland *had* shifted in the wake of Brexit and under Pedro Sánchez Spain now dropped the threat made by Rajoy to veto Scottish accession, stating that it would not oppose it so long as independence was achieved within the legal framework of the UK (*El Periódico de Catalunya* 30 June 2016, *El País* 21 November 2018). Thus, there was some movement in the international sphere, although not so much within Spain. Even after Sánchez formed a stable coalition Government in early 2019, there was little immediate follow-up to announcements of a Spanish dialogue with Catalonia, and then the COVID-19 pandemic caused further delay over the next two years.

Still betting on Brussels?

The official party discourses analysed in this chapter reveal how the messages articulated by Catalan pro-independence forces have changed over time, yet they provide somewhat limited guides to the assumptions and calculations that party elites make about the role that 'Europe' and European actors may play in the struggle to achieve a valid and effective self-determination process in Catalonia. Elite interviews, especially when undertaken at different stages of the independence push, provide more insights into the strategic thinking that has taken place among pro-independence elites and how this has evolved, partly in response to European reactions to the Catalan challenge. They are key to understanding why, in the face of EU negativity in response to Catalan efforts to stage an effective referendum, mainstream pro-independence parties have not changed their positions on European integration nor lost faith in the European project.

While European responses to the Catalan independence challenge certainly shifted in the years immediately after 2017, the tide was still far from having turned definitively. Although somewhat averse to engaging in overt self-criticism, pro-independence parties did have to come to terms with the setback and seek to learn from it. While insisting that October 2017 had produced a mandate of some kind, they implicitly recognized that another referendum, viewed more widely to be legitimate, would be necessary if they were to stand some chance of it being effective. By the eve of the Catalan elections of 2021, however, ERC and JxCat were far apart both on how to achieve such a referendum and what prerequisites it would need to be effective. The one unifying chorus, as they faced a strong challenge from the Catalan Socialists, were the demands for an amnesty, the return of exiles and the right to self-determination coming from the prisoners, irrespective of affiliation. While 'Europe' did not figure prominently in the political campaigns ahead of these Catalan elections, the analysis presented here suggests a growing sense among Catalan pro-independence forces that the EU might be failing to defend what they perceived to be fundamental rights, with this leading to more nuanced views on the benefits of EU membership, albeit not necessarily an increase in Eurosceptic attitudes.

References

Amnesty International (2019). *Spain: Analysis of the Supreme Court's ruling in the case of Catalan leaders.* Available at www.amnesty.org/en/documents/eur41/1393/2019/en/ (accessed 25 August 2021).

Aumaitre, Ariane (2017). Four graphs about Catalonia and citizens' attitudes towards the EU. *LSE blog, Euro Crisis in the Press*, 17 November. Available at https://blogs.lse.ac.uk/eurocrisispress/2017/11/17/four-graphs-about-catalonia-and-citizens-attitudes-towards-the-eu/ (accessed 25 August 2021).

Barrio, Astrid and Barberà, Òscar (2011). Convergència i Unió. In Anwen Elias and Filippo Tronconi (eds), *From protest to power: Autonomist parties and the challenge of representation.* Vienna: Braumüller.

Candidatura d'Unitat Popular (CUP) (2021). Programa Polític. *Un nou cicle per guanyar*, February. Available at https://perguanyar.cat/programa-politic/ (accessed 25 August 2021).

76 Catalonia

Cetrà, Daniel, and Liñeira, Robert (2018). Breaking-up within Europe: Substate nationalist strategies in multilevel polities. *Journal of Common Market Studies*, 56 (3): 717–729.

Crameri, Kathryn (2014). *'Goodbye, Spain?' The question of independence for Catalonia*. Eastbourne: Sussex Academic Press.

Crameri, Kathryn (2015). Political power and counterpower: The complex dynamics of the Catalan independence movement. *Nationalism and Ethnic Politics*, 21 (1): 104–120.

Dowling, Andrew (2013) *Catalonia since the Spanish Civil War: Reconstructing the nation*. Eastbourne: Sussex University Press.

Duerr, Glen M.E. (2015). *Secessionism and the European Union: The future of Flanders, Scotland and Catalonia*. Lanham, MD: Lexington Books.

Esquerra Republicana de Catalunya (ERC) (2019a). *Programa electoral, Eleccions a les Corts espanyoles. Va de llibertat*. Available at https://vadelli bertat.esquerra.cat/pdf/programa-corts-espanyoles-2019.pdf (accessed 25 August 2021).

Esquerra Republicana de Catalunya (ERC) (2019b). 28è Congrés Nacional. *Ponència política*. Available at www.esquerra.cat/arxius/28congresnacional/28cgn-ponencia-politica.pdf (accessed 25 August 2021).

Esquerra Republicana de Catalunya (ERC) (2021). *Eleccions al Parlament de Catalunya 2021, programa electoral. Al costat de la gent*. Available at www.esquerra.cat/alcostatdelagent/p2021-programa.pdf (accessed 25 August 2021).

European Commission (2017). *White Paper on the future of Europe*. Available at https://ec.europa.eu/info/future-europe/white-paper-future-europe/white-paper-future-europe-five-scenarios_en (accessed 25 August 2021).

Generalitat de Catalunya (2014). *Paths for Catalonia's integration in the European Union*. Barcelona: Generalitat de Catalunya.

Generalitat de Catalunya (2019). Ministry for Foreign Action, Institutional Relations and Transparency. *Europe Plan*, November. Available at https://exteriors.gencat.cat/en/ambits-dactuacio/afers_exteriors/ue/pla-europa/ (accessed 25 August 2021).

Gillespie, Richard (2017). Pro-sovereignty politics in Catalonia and the Basque Country: Are the two cases comparable? In Javier Muñoz-Basols, Laura Lonsdale and Manuel Delgado (eds), *The Routledge companion to Iberian studies*. London: Routledge.

Gray, Caroline (2020). *Territorial Politics and the Party System in Spain*. London: Routledge.

Junts pel Sí (2015). *Programa electoral*. Available at www.esquerra.cat/arxius/p rogrames/c2015_programa.pdf (accessed 25 August 2021).

Junts per Catalunya (JxCat) (2017). *Eleccions al Parlament de Catalunya, 21 de desembre de 2017: Programa electoral*. Available at https://ep00.epimg. net/descargables/2017/12/05/356c231f951070d42f5cddd84f72f8ef.pdf (accessed 25 August 2021).

Catalonia 77

Junts per Catalunya (JxCat) (2020). *Ponència política de Junts per Catalunya.* Available at www.juntsxamposta.cat/ponencia-politica-de-juntsxcatalunya -aprovada-el-congres-3-10-2020 (accessed 25 August 2021).

Junts per Catalunya (JxCat) (2021). *Eleccions al Parlament de Catalunya 2021, programa electoral.* Available at https://junts.cat/wp-content/uploads/2021/ 02/Programa-Electoral-JUNTS-14F.pdf (accessed 25 August 2021).

Muro, Diego, and Vlaskamp, Martijn (2016). How do prospects of EU membership influence support for secession? A survey experiment in Catalonia and Scotland. *West European Politics,* 39 (6): 1115–1138.

Nagel, Klaus-Jürgen (2014). ¿Del autonomismo al independentismo? En vías de interpreter el giro reciente del nacionalismo catalán. In Ferran Archilés i Cardona and Ismael Saz (eds), *Naciones y Estado: La cuestión española.* Valencia: Universitat de Valencia.

Strubell, Miquel (2013). Catalonia's self-determination process: A bottom-up movement? Conference on 'Self-determination processes in the EU: The case of Catalonia', organized by the European Institute, University College London and the Public Diplomacy Council of Catalonia, held at UCL, London, 25 October. Available at https://miquelstrubell.blogspot.com/sea rch?q=self-determination+processes (accessed 25 August 2021).

4 Scottish independence in an integrated Europe
Still seen as viable?

The pursuit of independence for Scotland by the Scottish National Party (SNP) is as old as the party itself (see Chapter 2 in this volume), but currently it is presenting the UK with one of its most severe constitutional challenges. The SNP has been in office in Scotland uninterruptedly since 2007, and at the same time as it has consolidated its position as Scotland's governing party it has taken a more confrontational stance against the UK Government, especially after Brexit. Even though the SNP's longstanding vision of 'Scottish independence in an integrated Europe' has not changed much in form, this chapter advances the argument that the SNP finds itself in a much more difficult political position than it has been in recent years when it comes to European affairs. This is because Brexit can be said to undo the party's carefully crafted gradualist discourse on national independence and European integration. The analysis in the chapter supports the argument that Brexit can be said to force the SNP to make a choice between two unions – the UK or the European Union (EU) – in the pursuit of independence. Before Brexit, the party could argue to its supporters and potential voters that Scotland did not have to choose. Post-Brexit, the SNP's vision of Scotland rejoining the EU as an independent country necessarily means that it would need to end the centuries-old union with the rest of the UK, with all what that would entail in terms of difficult political trade-offs and possibly erecting a border across the island of Great Britain.

SNP discourse on Europe and the Scottish referendum in 2014

The SNP won 69 seats in the Scottish elections of May 2011 and this resulted in the first majority government in Scotland since the devolved Scottish Parliament at Holyrood was inaugurated in 1999. It was a remarkable feat considering that the Scottish two-tier electoral

DOI: 10.4324/9781003129028-4

system can be said to have been designed precisely to make it hard for any party to achieve a parliamentary majority of its own (McTavish and Garnett 2020: 248). Moreover, ahead of the elections, opinion polls suggested that Labour had a significant lead over the SNP but Labour eventually ended up with only 37 seats, whereas the Conservatives garnered 15 seats and the Liberal Democrats a mere five (see Figure 4.1).

The SNP 2011 electoral manifesto clearly emphasized the need for Scotland to become an independent country in order to better promote the interests of Scottish society and to allow the people living in Scotland to decide on issues that matter to them 'in the same way as other countries' (SNP 2011: 28). National independence was to a large extent portrayed as a means to make Scotland more prosperous and at the same time more democratic as decisions could be taken that were more aligned with the needs and preferences of Scottish citizens. Overall, the tone in the manifesto was very much in keeping with the way in which the SNP had sought to legitimize Scottish independence claims since the late 1980s (see Chapter 2 in this volume). 'Europe' is referred to in the manifesto in relation to various policy issues, for instance as providing opportunities in terms of EU regional funds and to promote Scottish businesses and jobs in green energy. Interestingly, 'Europe' also plays a role in terms of proving a benchmark for progressive social policies favoured by the SNP, for example 'increase childcare support here in Scotland to match the best elsewhere in Europe' (SNP 2011: 22). The manifesto also claimed that the SNP will 'seek an enhanced role for Scotland in Europe' (ibid.: 29), and in a key passage it linked independence to how the SNP envisioned Scotland's relations with the UK (as a 'partnership of equals') and as a member

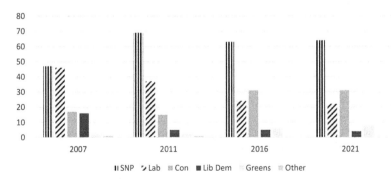

Figure 4.1 Scottish elections, 2007–2021
Note: Numbers represent seats in the Scottish Parliament.

80 *Scotland*

of the EU 'there will continue to be open borders, shared rights, free trade and extensive cooperation ... That is the reality of independence in this interdependent world' (ibid.: 28).

As a result of the 2011 Scottish elections, the SNP leader, Alex Salmond, remained in office as First Minister and one of the key objectives that the Scottish Government set out to achieve was to deliver on the promise to hold a referendum on independence. It has been suggested that the SNP leadership might have preferred to hold the referendum at a later point in time but since the party won a clear majority it was politically not feasible to postpone it, and the decision was most likely also facilitated by the fact that the SNP's political opponents thought that 'they could call the nationalists' bluff, score an easy victory, and see off the idea of independence for a long time' (Keating and McEwan 2017: 2). The Scottish Government set out to negotiate the legal basis for the referendum with the UK Government and in October 2012 the two parties signed the Edinburgh Agreement. The parties agreed to a so-called Section 30 procedure of the Scotland Act to allow for a single-question referendum on Scottish independence to be held before the end of 2014 and that the Scottish Parliament should legislate on the date and the rules for the referendum. Both governments agreed that the referendum should be overseen by an impartial electoral commission.

As the governments in Edinburgh and London had agreed on the modalities for the referendum, the SNP-led Scottish Government published a 650-page white paper on independence entitled *Scotland's Future*. The white paper set out to answer questions about what would happen to a range of policies and issues in the event that a majority of Scottish citizens voted 'yes' in the referendum, such as the economy, finance, health, education, justice and home affairs, the environment, democracy and human rights, and Scotland's international relations, including EU membership (Scottish Government 2013a). The white paper demonstrated that the Scottish Government perceived EU membership as being in the best interests of Scotland, and its '*natural position* is as an active participant in the EU, which provides us with unparalleled access to a market of over 500 million people' (ibid.: 216, emphasis added).

The white paper declared that following a vote for independence, the Scottish Government 'will immediately seek discussions with the Westminster Government, with member states and with the institutions of the EU to agree the process whereby a smooth transition to independent EU membership can take place on the day Scotland becomes an independent country' (Scottish Government 2013a: 220).

Scotland 81

However, it declared that an independent Scotland would not seek membership of the Eurozone or the Schengen Area, as it wanted Scotland to remain part of the Common Travel Area (CTA) with the UK and Ireland. The CTA was described in words that echoed the SNP 2011 manifesto, as an expression of a broader 'social union' which ties all nations on the islands of Britain and Ireland together in economic, social and cultural bonds (ibid.: 222–224). This was very much in keeping with Alex Salmond's vision that he set out in a series of speeches in 2013 suggesting that Scotland was actually a member of no less than six unions (i.e. political and economic union; social union; currency union; a union of the Crowns with the UK; a defence union through the North Atlantic Treaty Organization (NATO); and membership of the EU), and that independence would certainly not mean that Scotland would seek to leave all of them (Scottish Government 2013b).

Both sides of the political campaigns that preceded the 2014 referendum can be said to have made use of notions of 'Europe' to favour their respective positions. The 'Yes Scotland' campaign, headed by Blair Jenkins (formerly at BBC Scotland) and supported by the SNP, drew on the well-established SNP trope of independence in an integrated Europe to try to convince hesitant voters that a vote for an independent Scotland would not be a vote in favour of separatist rupture but rather a vote in favour of giving the people of Scotland the means to decide better on their future as an equal partner among other European countries. When the SNP manifesto for the 2014 European Parliament (EP) elections was launched in April of that year, Alex Salmond stressed that Scotland and the EU had been partners for over 40 years to the great benefit of Scottish businesses and jobs, but that this was 'threatened by the Westminster parties' obsessive anti-European agenda … We need the opportunity to speak with our own voice in Europe to build on the positive relationships with our neighbours Scotland has already established' (BBC 30 April 2014).

On the other side, the 'Better Together' campaign, headed by Alistair Darling (the former UK Chancellor) and supported by Labour, Conservatives and Liberal Democrats, argued that EU membership would not necessarily be automatic for an independent Scotland and that it was not certain that Scotland would be able to secure opt-outs from the Eurozone and the Schengen Area. In January 2014, the UK Government released its position on this matter in a *Scotland Analysis* paper and while it did not assert that Scotland would be rejected outright by the EU, it did emphasize that EU accession would most

82   Scotland

probably be cumbersome, uncertain and costly (UK Government 2014). Moreover, the Scottish Affairs Committee of the House of Commons insisted that an independent Scotland would have to reapply for EU membership under Article 49 of the Treaty on European Union (TEU), and that it would be outside of the EU for an indeterminate period of time and in a disadvantageous position while reaccession was negotiated (Keating 2017: 8).

But it was not only representatives of the UK Government and the 'Better Together' campaign who made these kinds of arguments ahead of the referendum. In early 2014, the President of the European Commission, José Manuel Durão Barroso, stated in an interview with the BBC that it would be 'extremely difficult, if not impossible' for an independent Scotland to remain within the EU (BBC 16 February 2014). Barroso's arguments resonated with the Prodi doctrine (see Chapter 1 in this volume) and in the interview he even referred to Spain's refusal to recognize Kosovo as an issue that would make it difficult for Scotland to join the EU. Jean-Claude Juncker, who succeeded Barroso in that same year, later made a comment that EU enlargement in the Western Balkans was unlikely to be on the table in the foreseeable future. This stance was subsequently used by supporters of the 'no' side, such as Ruth Davidson (the leader of the Scottish Conservative Party) to say that the door would remain closed to Scottish EU membership, although Juncker's office quickly denied that there were any links between Scotland and the Balkans in this regard (Keating 2017: 4).

The uncertainties surrounding Scottish independence and EU membership were not only spurred by political rhetoric during the campaign but also arose from what seemed to be genuine disagreements among legal scholars and practitioners. For example, the former British judge at the Court of Justice of the European Union (CJEU), Sir David Edward, had argued in favour of the use of Article 48 TEU and subsequent treaty change to allow the EU to recognize Scotland as a member state with continuity of effect (Edward 2012). However, other legal scholars and EU officials were supportive of the UK Government's position or at least advanced the argument that there was no clear precedent in EU law and that the matter would probably and eventually be decided by the CJEU (Kenealy 2014).

The referendum was held on 18 September 2014 and 55 per cent of the participating voters said 'no' to the question 'should Scotland be an independent country?' The turnout was almost 85 per cent of the registered voters which obviously is a high number by any comparison. Alex Salmond resigned following the defeat and Nicola Sturgeon

Scotland 83

was elected SNP leader and appointed as First Minister of Scotland. Soon after the referendum, the UK Government declared that an all-party commission, chaired by Lord Robert Smith of Kelvin, would oversee the implementation of new devolved powers to Scotland in honour of a pledge made by the Conservatives, Labour and the Liberal Democrats just before the referendum. All five parties in the Scottish Parliament were represented in the Smith Commission and the bill devolving further powers was passed unanimously by the Scottish Parliament in March 2016.

The road to Brexit and the SNP's constitutional challenge

The defeat in the 2014 referendum did not result in the SNP losing its leading position in Scottish politics – quite the contrary. In the 2015 UK general election, the SNP won a landslide of 56 seats out of the 59 Scottish seats, whereas Labour, the Conservatives and the Liberal Democrats only won one seat each. This also meant that the SNP became the third largest party in the House of Commons. The SNP 2015 electoral manifesto focused more on advancing Scotland's interests within the UK, rather than arguing in favour of independence. For instance, the manifesto stated that the SNP would focus on 'sorting [out] the broken Westminster system' and 'delivering home rule for Scotland' (SNP 2015: 35).

However, as the Conservatives had won an overall majority in the UK general election, Prime Minister David Cameron had no choice other than to make good on his pre-election promise to hold a referendum on the UK's membership of the EU. It was decided that it should be held in June 2016. The 'Britain Stronger in Europe' campaign was endorsed by Cameron as well as by leading figures in the Conservative Party, including Home Secretary Theresa May, alongside Labour, the SNP, the Greens and Plaid Cymru in Wales. The 'Vote Leave' campaign was endorsed by the Eurosceptic Member of the EP (MEP) Nigel Farage and the UK Independence Party (UKIP) as well as prominent Conservative politicians, such as Boris Johnson and Michael Gove (but also some Labour politicians). In early 2016 the 'Scotland Stronger in Europe' campaign, headed by Professor Mona Siddiqui and endorsed by all the parties in the Scottish Parliament, was launched. Interestingly, the long-time independence champion and SNP veteran, Jim Sillars, announced that he would not support 'remain' since he thought that the EU was 'a profoundly undemocratic organization' and that the SNP should not 'tell our supporters to vote to remain in it' (BBC 21 January 2016).[1]

84 Scotland

The Scottish elections in May 2016 were held one and a half months before the UK referendum on EU membership. The SNP won 63 seats in the Scottish Parliament and although this fell two seats short of a parliamentary majority, the party could still form a minority government and SNP leader Nicola Sturgeon could carry on in office (see Figure 4.1). The Scottish Conservatives under Ruth Davidson's leadership become the second largest party in the Scottish Parliament which meant that it surpassed Labour, which had never happened before in the Scottish Parliament. The SNP 2016 electoral manifesto laid out a progressive vision for Scotland as a fairer and wealthier country, and it stated that the SNP would 'campaign passionately and positively for an "in" vote, to remain in the EU' (SNP 2016: 41). The manifesto stated that the SNP hoped and believed that citizens in the UK and Scotland would vote to remain in the EU but that it did not take anything for granted. In terms of the SNP's vision of Scotland's place in 'Europe', the manifesto stated that EU membership mattered to Scotland as it meant having 'direct access to the world's biggest single market for goods and services' (ibid.). Being a member of the EU had already led to improved workers' rights and parental leave. EU membership is ultimately 'about being part of a family of nations founded on the principles of peace, democracy and human rights, promoting and fostering co-operation to tackle complex international problems' (ibid.).

Besides highlighting the economic and political benefits of EU membership, prior to the 2016 referendum the SNP had already alluded to the constitutional crisis that would be provoked if the UK should withdraw from the EU. The 2016 manifesto declared that the SNP believed that the Scottish Parliament should have the right to hold another referendum if independence became the preferred option for a majority of the Scottish people or if Scotland were 'taken out of the EU against our will' (SNP 2016: 24). In the SNP 2015 manifesto, the party had claimed that it would oppose UK withdrawal from the EU and 'would propose that, in any future referendum there should be a double majority requirement. Each of the four constituent nations of the UK would have to vote for withdrawal before the UK as a whole could leave the EU' (SNP 2015: 18). It stated that the SNP wanted to see a greater role for devolved administrations in the EU Council of Ministers and that it would seek an agreement with the UK Government on speaking rights for Scottish ministers and direct Scottish input into the development of UK policy on key EU issues (ibid.: 19). In a speech in Brussels in June 2015, Sturgeon also emphasized the need to achieve a 'double majority' before the UK

Scotland 85

could leave EU due to the fact that the UK was a multinational state, implying that a majority of English citizens should not be allowed to decide over a majority of Scottish citizens on such an important matter (BBC 2 June 2015).

However, that is what transpired on 23 June 2016, as 52 per cent of the citizens who participated in the Brexit referendum voted that the UK should leave the EU, although 62 per cent of Scottish voters voted in favour of remaining in the EU (a majority in Northern Ireland also voted in favour of 'remain'). The turnout at the UK-wide referendum was 72 per cent (slightly lower in Scotland at 67 per cent). David Cameron resigned immediately after the referendum and Theresa May took over as leader of the Conservative Party and as UK Prime Minister. Sturgeon travelled to Brussels just days after the referendum to meet with the Presidents of the European Commission and the EP, Jean-Claude Juncker and Martin Schulz, as well as the leader of the Alliance of Liberals and Democrats for Europe group in the EP, Guy Verhofstadt. Her mission was to make it clear to the European audience that the Scots had voted differently to the UK as a whole and that 'there is an aspiration and desire in Scotland ... to protect Scotland's relationship with the EU and our place in the EU' (*The Guardian* 29 June 2016). However, the French President, François Hollande, and the Spanish Prime Minister, Mariano Rajoy, responded that Scotland had no competence to negotiate with the EU (BBC 29 June 2016).

Before the negotiations between the EU and the UK on the terms for the British withdrawal from the Union started, in December 2016 the Scottish Government published a report entitled *Scotland's Place in Europe* which laid out its vision of what kind of Brexit it preferred. This included the hope that the UK should avoid a 'hard Brexit' and remain in the EU's Common Market and Customs Union, even though Sturgeon emphasized in the Foreword that her preferred option for Scotland would be to become a full member of the EU as an independent country (Scottish Government 2016: vi). The report also stated that the Scottish Government would seek to secure a range of powers being repatriated to Scotland, powers that would be transferred back to the UK from the EU as a result of Brexit. The overall tone in the 2016 report was that the Scottish Government was ready to compromise to protect Scottish interests in a difficult situation that it had not chosen for itself.

However, the UK Government did not concede. Moreover, the UK Supreme Court's ruling on the UK Government's right to trigger Article 50 TEU to initiate the negotiations on the British withdrawal stipulated that the UK Government needed authorization by an Act of Parliament, but not by the Scottish Parliament since the Court did

86 Scotland

not consider it to be a sovereign parliament as its powers are devolved from Westminster (BBC 24 January 2017). In response to these actions, which the SNP deemed not to cater to Scotland's interests, Sturgeon indicated that the Scottish Government might want to organize a second referendum on independence before the Brexit negotiations were completed, but Theresa May rejected the proposal on the grounds that 'now is not the time', although she did suggest that such a referendum might indeed be contemplated once Brexit had been completed (BBC 27 March 2017).

Soon after Article 50 TEU was enacted, May announced that the UK Government would seek to hold elections in June 2017, a decision probably informed by the strong support for the Conservatives in the polls at the time and the need to secure an even stronger parliamentary position to ratify a future EU-UK withdrawal agreement. But the plans backfired as the Conservative Party ended up losing its parliamentary majority and May had to rely on the Northern Irish, and staunchly unionist, Democratic Unionist Party (DUP) for support. Labour did not win the election, but achieved a slightly better result than in 2015. The SNP, however, lost 21 seats and ended up with 35. Nonetheless, the SNP retained its position as the largest Scottish party in the UK Parliament. Interestingly, as the Conservatives won more seats (13) than Labour (seven) in Scotland, the election results in 2017 seemed to reinforce the image that while the SNP was becoming the main opposition to the Conservatives in UK politics, the Conservatives were becoming the main opposition to the SNP in Scotland.

That the SNP wanted to present itself as the 'real' opposition to the Conservatives in the UK was evident in the SNP 2017 electoral manifesto. The main message was that the SNP would work to promote a fairer, wealthier and greener society. It stated that even though the election was not about Scottish independence it was still very much about Scotland's future. The SNP declared that it opposed the UK Government's 'hard line' on Brexit. Echoing in large parts the Scottish Government's 2016 report, it proposed that the UK should remain as part of the Common Market as 'there is no rational case for taking Scotland, or the UK, out of [it]' (SNP 2017: 22). The manifesto stated that Scotland, after the outcome of the Brexit process, should have 'a real choice about our future' (ibid.: 29). The SNP also argued that the 2016 Scottish elections had delivered a 'democratic mandate' for an independence referendum, given that the UK's withdrawal from the EU now seemed inevitable and that it would be 'democratically unsustainable' to block the people of Scotland from having a choice about their future (ibid.).

In terms of its vision for Scotland's place in 'Europe', the manifesto maintained that 'if Scotland chooses to become independent, we should be a member state of the EU' (SNP 2017: 29). It promised that, as an independent country and a member of the EU, Scotland would seek to reform the Common Fisheries Policy to better serve the interests of the Scottish fisheries industry, suggesting that this was something that the UK Government had never done. But leaving the EU as a result of Brexit was said to also pose non-economic risks to citizens in Scotland since it was not clear whether or not the UK would seek to withdraw from the European Convention on Human Rights. The 2017 manifesto referred to the 2016 Scottish Government report as a 'compromise proposal' that had been presented to the UK Government, but which had been 'rejected out of hand' (ibid.: 30). The SNP therefore argued that if it won the election in Scotland, this would 'give us a mandate to demand a place for Scotland at the Brexit negotiating table and the inclusion of the case for our place in the Single Market in the UK's negotiating remit' (ibid.).

EU-UK negotiations on the terms for the UK's withdrawal were initiated in June 2017, with the UK Government in a much more precarious political position than before the general election as it had to rely on the DUP for parliamentary support. This meant that the post-Brexit status of Northern Ireland became possibly even more difficult to solve, even though there was a range of other contentious issues as well, such as the status of EU citizens in the UK, trade rules and tariffs, and migration. Not surprisingly, the negotiations between the UK and the EU turned out to be very difficult (on the Brexit negotiations, see among others Biermann and Jagdhuber 2021; Figueira and Martill 2021; Diamond et al. 2018; Hix 2018). In early 2019, Theresa May failed to get the first negotiated agreement with the EU ratified by the UK Parliament. Before that, leading Conservative politicians had criticized May's deal for not delivering a 'hard enough' Brexit. For example, David Davis (the UK's chief negotiator) and Boris Johnson (UK Foreign Secretary) had left their cabinet positions months earlier. The Scottish Government also criticized the first agreement, but for being 'too hard' as it fundamentally amounted to a free trade agreement which it felt would negatively affect EU-UK trade, economic growth and jobs in Scotland (Scottish Government 2018). Moreover, it stressed that the UK Government had not granted Edinburgh any role in the negotiations and had rejected the possibility of seeking a different relationship for Scotland with the EU, although it had done so for Northern Ireland (ibid.).

88 Scotland

Doing Brexit, undoing the UK?

Several attempts were made by the UK Government to ratify the first withdrawal agreement before the initial deadline expired in March 2019, but to no avail. The failure was partly due to the spilt within the Conservatives on how 'hard' a version of Brexit they should seek and partly due to the failure of Theresa May to secure enough parliamentary support for the agreement that her Government had managed to negotiate with Brussels. The European Council eventually decided to extend the deadline until 31 October. May announced her resignation in April and Boris Johnson took over as party leader and as UK Prime Minister. Johnson announced that his Government would seek to renegotiate the agreement with the EU but that he was prepared for the UK to leave the EU without one (the so-called no deal scenario). The UK Parliament moved to prevent this from happening by way of passing legislation that was meant to prohibit the British Government from seeking such a solution. In October, the UK and the EU managed to agree on a new withdrawal agreement. The European Council then agreed to yet another extension to the deadline until 31 January 2020 and Johnson's Government managed to secure parliamentary support for a UK general election to be held on 12 December.

Since the initial deadline had been extended, the UK participated in the elections to the EP in June 2019. Brexit was, of course, the main campaign question and in many ways this election was seen as a stand-in second Brexit referendum which benefited the parties that articulated clear positions on the issue of Brexit and the UK's future relations with the EU (Curtice 2019). Nigel Farage's new Brexit party won a total of 29 seats, whereas the Conservatives only garnered four seats (–15). The distinctively pro-EU Liberal Democrats won 16 seats (+15), but the more ambiguous Labour garnered 10 seats (–10). The SNP won three of Scotland's six MEPs, although it should be mentioned that Farage's Brexit party won one MEP 'north of the border' (and UKIP had won one Scottish MEP in the EP elections in 2014). The SNP 2019 European manifesto stated that it would work to 'stop Brexit' and prevent a 'no deal', and in general it outlined a series of benefits that EU membership accorded to Scotland in terms of economic opportunities, enhanced rights, free movement, opportunities for cooperation and so on (SNP 2019a). The manifesto also argued that Brexit and the way that the UK Government handled the issue clearly showed that Scotland needed to become independent to be in control of its own destiny as a 'normal' European country. In the SNP's discourse, Scottish independence was starting to be framed as a

Scotland 89

means of undoing Brexit and allowing Scotland to become 'one of the EU's small independent nations' (ibid.: 4). Sharing sovereignty was what 'normal' European countries had learnt to do as a result of decades of European integration, and the SNP maintained that Scotland would stand a better chance of being treated with respect as a member of the EU rather than as part of the UK (ibid.).

In December 2019, a general election was held in the UK. The Conservatives campaigned under the slogan 'Get Brexit done' and the party won 365 seats (+48) which meant that Johnson secured a comfortable parliamentary majority (see Figure 4.2). The SNP won 48 Scottish seats (+13), which was quickly portrayed by Sturgeon as a vindication of its persistent criticism of the UK Government: 'Scotland has sent a very clear message: we don't want a Boris Johnson government, we don't want to leave the EU', she declared (BBC 13 December 2019). The key pledges in the SNP 2019 manifesto resonated broadly with many of the progressive positions that the party had advanced in recent years, such as working to make Scotland fairer, wealthier and greener. But it was clear that the main concern for the SNP at this election was Brexit and its effects on Scotland. According to the SNP, the way in which the British Government had handled this complex issue clearly showed just how broken the Westminster system was. The UK's 'democratic deficit' was articulated in terms of it being said to rest on an 'unequal partnership'.

> Wales and England both voted to leave and under the Boris Johnson deal will leave. Northern Ireland is to get a special deal and the right to choose its future. Scotland – the nation of the UK with the highest remain vote – is to get nothing.
>
> (SNP 2019b: 6)

The issue of a second independence referendum was also emphasized in the SNP manifesto. It argued that there was 'a clear mandate to hold a referendum' but that the process needed to be legal which was why the manifesto emphasized that the SNP would seek to achieve the necessary transfer of power from London (SNP 2019b: 10). The manifesto presented this as being a question of democracy and argued that it would be 'unsustainable' for the UK Government to deny the Scottish Parliament the right to decide on a referendum, especially in the event of an 'SNP election victory'. The manifesto stressed the need for a legal and agreed process so that the legitimacy of a future referendum could not be questioned in Scotland or elsewhere; an insistence that should be understood against the

90 *Scotland*

background of the events that took place in Catalonia in the aftermath of the unconstitutional 'referendum' in 2017 (see Chapter 3 in this volume). Concerns about the views of the European audience were particularly pronounced as the manifesto underscored that for 'EU member states in particular, it will be essential to demonstrate that a referendum has been held legally and constitutionally' (ibid.).

It is particularly interesting in the context of this chapter that the manifesto can be said to portray EU membership as being what 'normal' European countries strive for in order to seek cooperative solutions to common problems. This view obviously is meant to stand in stark contrast to the UK Government's vision of seeking a future outside of the EU. The SNP argued that '12 of the other 27 EU member states have populations similar to or smaller than Scotland. For countries of our size the attractions of being part of the world's biggest trading block and single market are obvious' (SNP 2019b: 11). Ireland is referred to as a successful example, and the manifesto suggested that Scotland's energy resources, climate leadership and universities, among other things, implied that Scotland would not only contribute to the EU, but would also gain a great deal from it (ibid.). By late 2019, it was clear that the SNP was keen to depict Brexit not only as damaging to Scottish economic interests, but as something of an aberration in modern European politics, which at the same time revealed that the UK's current constitutional arrangement was not working for Scotland.

Scottish independence and integration in Europe post-Brexit

After the UK finally withdrew from the EU on 31 January 2020, Nicola Sturgeon issued a statement:

> We are asking our friends in Europe to leave a light on for Scotland so we can find our way home [since] being part of the EU is an expression of shared values we hold dear, the ideas of solidarity, openness and a genuine partnership of equal nations.
>
> (SNP 2020)

The withdrawal meant the start of an 11-month transition period in which a new EU-UK agreement was meant to be negotiated, including sensitive issues such as the future status of Northern Ireland. However, those negotiations quickly faced additional difficulties following the outbreak of the coronavirus (COVID-19) pandemic in early 2020. European countries such as Italy and Spain were badly affected from

Scotland 91

the outset, while the UK saw the number of infected people increase rapidly by March. In the UK, the handling of the pandemic, with the introduction of prolonged periods of lockdown and restrictions to slow the spread of the virus, took place in the context of a looming constitutional crisis spurred by Brexit and the SNP's stance on Scottish independence. For much of 2020 it looked as if the UK Government's handling of the pandemic would play to the SNP's advantage by providing citizens with yet another reason as to why Scotland needed to be independent, but that started to change in early 2021 as the UK's vaccination programme appeared more successful than those of most other EU member states.

Against this backdrop the 2021 elections to the Scottish Parliament were held. They were the first to be held in the UK since the outbreak of the COVID-19 pandemic, and elections were also held to the Welsh Parliament as well as to local councils in England. Labour performed well in Wales and in major English cities, whereas the Conservatives did well across England and its candidate even won the Hartlepool by-election (traditionally a Labour stronghold). In Scotland, the SNP won 64 seats and fell just one seat short of securing a parliamentary majority of its own (see Figure 4.1). The Conservatives (+/–0), Labour (–2) and the Liberal Democrats (–1) more or less held on to the same number of seats as 2016, although the Scottish Greens won eight seats (+2) which meant that the pro-independence parties together secured a majority. For the SNP, the elections were preceded by mounting pressure from activists to push ahead with a second independence referendum, as well as the launch of Alex Salmond's new pro-independence Alba Party ('Scotland' in Gaelic). The run-up to Salmond's move was an investigation against him regarding sexual harassment that had led him to resign from the SNP and take the Scottish Government to court on the charge of abuse of process. This soon became a problem also for Sturgeon as she was accused of having misled members of the Scottish Parliament about what and when she knew about the accusations; she lost face when the High Court in Edinburgh acquitted Salmond of all charges on 23 March 2020.

In late March 2021, an independent inquiry found that Sturgeon had not breached the ministerial code (BBC 22 March 2021), although a Scottish parliamentary inquiry found that the Scottish Government's handling of the matter had 'fundamental errors' (BBC 23 March 2021). The latter inquiry led the Conservatives to table a motion of no confidence against Sturgeon, but it was rejected by the SNP and Greens (Labour and the Liberal Democrats abstained). Soon afterwards, possibly seeking to tap into perceived grassroots frustration

92   Scotland

with the SNP's more cautious strategy, Salmond announced that the Alba Party would stand in the 2021 Scottish elections with the aim of building a 'supermajority for independence' (BBC 26 March 2021). Although the Alba Party did not win any seats, its launch seemed to suggest that the electoral competition for Scottish pro-independence voters might involve more actors in the future.

One notable aspect of Salmond's political rhetoric ahead of the 2021 election was his accusations that the current SNP leadership devoted too much attention to issues of gender equality and green transformation, which seemed to signal that he aimed to exploit controversies surrounding 'woke' issues among certain Scottish voters (Scothorne 2021). Some pro-independence supporters might perhaps be susceptible to such political rhetoric, but if that was the case then the Alba Party nonetheless failed to capitalize on it at this point in time. Another short-term effect seemed to have been that as a result of some high-profile defections from the SNP to the Alba Party, such as MPs Kenny MacAskill and Neale Hanvey, Sturgeon and the SNP party leadership seemed to have been relieved of a number of internal vocal critics. But there is one aspect of the Alba Party that might prove more damaging to the SNP in the longer run. Some observers have suggested that the Alba Party's political position on issues such as currency and EU membership actually make more sense post-Brexit that the SNP's position (Thompson 2021). It seems very unlikely that Scotland could rejoin the EU and keep the British pound. In fact, it might be that setting up a Scottish currency and seeking membership of the European Free Trade Association, while retaining the UK currency and remaining in the customs unions and the Common Travel Area, would be more feasible, at least initially. Scottish citizens could then be offered a vote in a referendum, after independence had been achieved, on whether they wanted Scotland to apply for EU membership (ibid.).

The question of Scottish independence was placed at the centre of the SNP 2021 manifesto, closely connected to the party's explicitly progressive vision of wanting to promote a more prosperous, fair and sustainable Scottish society. However, the COVID-19 pandemic was present throughout the whole manifesto, and various proposals were related to post-pandemic recovery and handling the balancing act of reopening the economy and supressing the virus. For example, it claimed that NHS spending should be increased and that NHS staff should receive higher wages than those offered by the Conservatives (SNP 2021: 19–20). The pandemic was built into the SNP's discourse on independence as the party was arguing that, while its first priority

Scotland 93

was managing the pandemic, it would resume the work of preparing for a second referendum 'once the Covid crisis has passed' (ibid.: 12). The manifesto claimed that if the SNP was returned to power it would present a bill on a second independence referendum to the Scottish Parliament. However, it stated that any referendum must be 'capable of bringing about independence' and as such it needed to be seen as 'legitimate and constitutional at home and abroad' (ibid.). Given these prerequisites (and with the Catalan conflict still unresolved at the time), the SNP said that it would seek a negotiated solution with the UK Government on the basis of the 2014 referendum, and declared that it was 'undemocratic and unsustainable' for Westminster to refuse it (ibid.). However, should the UK Government block a future referendum bill by legal means, then the SNP would be ready to 'vigorously defend the [Scottish] Parliament's will in order to protect the democratic rights of the Scottish people' (ibid.).

In relation to visions of Scottish independence and European integration, the SNP 2021 manifesto referred to this relationship very much in the same ways as previous manifestos and reports analysed in this chapter. 'Europe' was said to provide various opportunities for Scottish society and in the SNP's discourse, Scotland was presented as deprived of these opportunities as a result of a choice it did not make for itself, while independence would secure its citizens 'the right to escape Brexit' (SNP 2021: 12). The SNP's vision of an independent Scotland was explicitly linked to the idea that national independence and European integration go hand in hand. It is what the 'wealthiest, fairest and happiest' European countries of Scotland's size are striving for, and if 'they can do it, why not Scotland?'. The manifesto set out the stark difference between the political project that the Conservatives and pro-Brexit forces in England envisioned for the UK, and the party's self-proclaimed progressive vision for Scotland, while laying out the main strategic outlook vis-à-vis 'Europe'. The SNP-led Scottish Government would

> prepare to rejoin the EU by keeping a close relationship with Europe. We will strengthen our Brussels base and make Scotland House the hub of our diplomatic representation across Europe. We will also expand our international network by establishing new innovations and investment hubs for the Nordic and Baltic regions.
>
> (Ibid.: 72).

94 *Scotland*

The SNP leadership and Scottish public opinion post-Brexit

The analysis above suggests that the SNP has not made drastic changes to its discourse on Scottish independence in an integrated Europe since 2010, but as a result of Brexit it can be said to be less concerned with toning down separatist features and more keen on emphasizing independence as a means to protect Scottish democracy and Scotland's place in Europe. There are indications that Scottish public opinion has swung in favour of independence in the immediate post-Brexit phase. For example, data from the 2019 Scottish Social Attitudes survey suggest that 'the pursuit of Brexit has served to weaken the perceived merits of the [UK] Union in the eyes of a modest but significant body of voters north of the border' (Curtice and Montagu 2020: 20). Semi-structured interviews with leading members of the SNP conducted in 2020–2021 suggest that Brexit is seen as being mainly beneficial for the party and the independence cause.

To start with, there is a perceived change of opinion towards Scotland in the rest of the EU as a result of Brexit (interviews SNP 1; SNP 2; SNP 3). Before 2016, Scottish independence was seen by mainstream European politicians as a somewhat annoying, quixotic project with little or no practical relevance, but since Brexit much more supportive tunes have allegedly been heard in Brussels and elsewhere. This view appears to be in keeping with the reception that Nicola Sturgeon received by high-ranking representatives of EU institutions in June 2016 (see above). The normal thing in Europe today is to be an EU member state and it is thus the UK that is doing something less normal. In fact, Brexit is seen as 'normalizing' Scottish independence claims in the eyes of other EU member states (interview SNP 3). Moreover, the idea of a Spanish veto on Scottish accession to the EU is not credible, so long as Scottish independence is the result of a negotiated solution within the framework of the UK's constitutional arrangements (interview SNP 1). That might of course depend on who is in power in Madrid, but at least the former Spanish Minister of Foreign Affairs and member of the Partido Socialista Obrero Español, Josep Borrell, has publicly stated that Spain would not oppose Scotland's bid for EU membership (*The Times* 21 November 2018).

According to one interviewee, it has helped that the SNP has explicitly stated that membership of the EU and NATO should be the 'cornerstones of Scottish independence' and while some on the left in Scotland still want to leave the EU altogether the SNP looks to Ireland and Denmark and considers that full EU membership but with some opt-outs would be the best option (interview SNP 1). It is also

Scotland 95

clear that the SNP seeks independence in order to join a bigger constellation rather than standing alone (interviews SNP 1; SNP 3). Scottish people generally have positive experiences of EU membership and multi-level governance after decades of European integration and devolution within the UK (ibid.). Another interviewee said that Brexit has meant that there is a much greater focus on the importance of the EU for Scotland both within the SNP and in Scottish society as a whole (interview SNP 2). This has also meant that the party's discourse on the EU in the period following the 2016 referendum was increasingly centred on the theme of 'what was taken away from Scottish citizens' as a result of Brexit (interview SNP 1).

One interviewee stressed that for many people in Scotland it was hard to disregard the fact that the UK Government claimed before the 2014 independence referendum that it was likely that Scotland would be forced out of the EU if the Scottish people voted for independence, and that Scotland would be given more devolved powers if it stayed within the UK (interview SNP 2). However, the tables have been turned since Brexit has forced Scotland out of the EU and it is possible that Scotland's regional autonomy will be reduced. A sense of helplessness is felt by many people in Scotland, according to this interviewee, who added that if Scotland is to be a modern, progressive and democratic country it needs to be in the EU (ibid.). The way in which Brexit has been carried out thus far has revealed to people in Scotland and Europe that the UK's self-image of being a multinational state does not correspond to reality (interview SNP 3). The idea of 'ultimate sovereignty' was something that English 'Brexiteers' were obsessed with, whereas people in Scotland were generally more relaxed about the idea of sharing sovereignty with other European countries (ibid.).

SNP members acknowledged that Scottish independence and EU membership still entail several 'tricky issues' in the post-Brexit setting (interviews SNP 1; SNP 2; SNP 3). Currency and fisheries were intensely debated in 2014 and are still seen as contentious issues, but the Smith Commission suggested that the Scottish fisheries industry would be better off inside the EU and as a member state Scotland would be capable of negotiating for Scottish interests. One interviewee stressed that although many difficult questions remain there is little doubt that when it comes to protecting opportunities for young people as well as the rights of EU citizens who live and work in Scotland there is no question that it would be better for Scotland to be inside rather than outside of the EU. The same goes for cooperating on efforts to mitigate climate change (interview SNP 2). The question of a

96 *Scotland*

border between Scotland and England was seen as particularly problematic. The difficulties surrounding the question of how to solve the border between Ireland, Northern Ireland, the UK and the EU is an important precedent in this context (interview SNP 3). Another interviewee nonetheless suggested that issues relating to trade tariffs and regulations will be difficult, but that the bottom line was still 'we'll work it out' (interview SNP 1).

It seems likely that the Scottish Government will be pressed to seek an agreement for a second independence referendum with the UK Government before the next Scottish elections (scheduled for 2026). In the event that London does not concede, it seems likely that Edinburgh would seek to take the case to the UK Supreme Court rather than pursue a unilateral and unconstitutional route as the Catalan Government under Carles Puigdemont did in 2017 (see Chapter 3 in this volume). SNP members emphasized that the party has always pursued independence within the boundaries of the rule of law (interviews SNP 1; SNP 3). SNP members seem to be very aware that governments and citizens in EU member states would not respond favourably to unconstitutional moves, and that the EU's position on independence claims continues to be that they are seen as matters of 'internal affairs' for sovereign states to deal with according to their constitutional arrangements (interview SNP 3). Party discipline will therefore be decisive, especially if there is widespread perception that the demand for a second referendum is high but London refuses to negotiate. A second independence referendum would be very different from the first, and people in Scotland agree with this because 'Brexit has changed everything' (ibid.).

It might be that the SNP's vision of independence and European integration post-Brexit resonates broadly with how Scottish citizens perceive the EU. However, Curtice and Montagu (2020) suggest that opinion data reveal that Eurosceptic attitudes are in fact relatively persistent in Scotland (see Figure 4.2). It is not inconceivable that there is a gap between the SNP leadership and Scottish public opinion in relation to the perceived costs and benefits of EU membership. There might be divergent levels of emotional attachment to the notion of belonging to Europe rather than to Britain across different demographic groups in Scottish society. It could also be that a position on EU membership similar to the one articulated by Alex Salmond's Alba Party (see above) might gain increased electoral support over time as Scottish citizens become accustomed to life outside of the EU.

Muro and Vlaskamp (2016) have shown that the risk of losing EU membership did not seem to have much of an effect on the opinion for

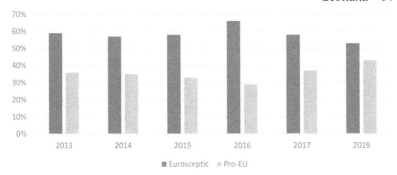

Figure 4.2 Public attitudes towards the EU in Scotland, 2013–2021
Note: 'Eurosceptic' denotes the combination of respondents answering that the UK should leave the EU or want to reduce its powers; 'Pro-EU' denotes the combination of respondents answering that the EU's powers should be kept as they are, should be expanded or that the UK should strive for the creation of a single European government.
Source: Curtice and Montagu (2020).

or against independence in Scotland. They did, however, find support for the notion that it depends on how strongly individuals feel that they belong to Scotland and how much they trust the EU to begin with. In their sample, it was only individuals who felt that they were as much Scottish as British and also had a high level of trust in the EU who seemed likely to reduce their support for independence if it came at the cost of losing EU membership. For those individuals who only felt Scottish and had low levels of trust in the EU, the loss of EU membership did not seem to matter very much at all, which seems to be consistent with more recent Scottish public opinion data (Curtice and Montagu 2020).

For some respondents, support for independence increased if it entailed Scotland leaving the EU (Muro and Vlaskamp 2016). This is an interesting finding in the context of this chapter since the combination of pro-independence and Eurosceptic attitudes seem to have been more prevalent in Scotland than in Catalonia, at least prior to the Brexit referendum in 2016 and the Catalan 'referendum' in 2017 (ibid.). However, in Scotland it seems that Brexit has led to an increase in the support for independence among people with high levels of trust in the EU and emotional attachment to both Scotland and the UK, which might have made them hesitant about independence in 2014 but less so after Brexit (Curtice and Montagu 2020).

98 *Scotland*

A choice between two unions?

According to the analysis presented above, the SNP's longstanding discourse in which Scottish independence and European integration are depicted as mutually reinforcing has not changed much. The party persistently holds up a particular vision of 'Europe' as an inspiration for a self-ascribed progressive political force such as the SNP. Based on manifestos, reports, statements and interview data, the practice of consistently highlighting Scotland's European identity appears to be used as a means to signal to people in Scotland and beyond that the SNP wants Scottish society to move towards something resembling an idealized version of Scandinavian-style social democracy. At the same time, the SNP emphasizes that Scotland is different from the rest of the UK, in particular England, in terms of its political values and aspirations. The SNP has stressed these aspects both before and since Brexit, which in the SNP discourse is depicted as harmful to both Scottish interests and democracy.

However, the analysis in this chapter also suggests that when Scottish opinion data on independence and EU membership are analysed it actually appears as if the SNP might now find itself in a much more difficult political situation than it has been in recent years when it comes to European affairs. This is because Brexit threatens the party's carefully crafted gradualist discourse on national independence and European integration. The SNP is now being forced to make a choice between one of two unions – the UK or the EU – in the pursuit of independence, and this makes it impossible for the party to convince supporters and potential voters that Scotland does not have to choose. In the post-Brexit setting, the SNP's vision of Scotland rejoining the EU as an independent country necessarily means that Scotland needs to end the union with the rest of the UK, which in all likelihood requires the creation of a Scottish currency as well as a border on the island of Great Britain.

It is not difficult to understand why the SNP still wants to highlight the intimate relationship between national independence and European integration, and why leading SNP members portray Brexit as an aberration in contemporary European politics, because doing so makes it possible to depict EU membership as a stepping stone towards making an independent Scotland 'viable' as a normal European state (see Chapter 1 in this volume). But the strategic dilemma for the SNP seems to be that emphasizing the need to rejoin the EU and recover 'Scotland's place in Europe' might not be prioritized among the voters that the SNP and other pro-independence parties would need to convince to broaden the public support in favour of

Scotland 99

independence. The SNP seems to have been doing quite well since 2016 in terms of articulating many Scottish citizens' frustration with the UK Government's handling of Brexit, but it might still be the case that ultimately a majority of Scottish citizens will favour the UK over the EU. In sum, they might prefer to lend electoral support to those who claim to change Westminster and reform the UK rather than to those who struggle to have a Scottish Prime Minister present at European Council meetings in Brussels.

Thus, 'Europe' can be said to have become potentially a more divisive issue in Scottish politics, even though a majority of Scottish voters voted in favour of remaining in the EU in the 2016 referendum. This might make it harder for the SNP to use the notion of belonging to Europe in order to secure broader public support for Scottish independence, which is necessary to achieve this enduring national aspiration. Brexit has nonetheless made it possible for the SNP to forcefully argue that the UK's constitutional arrangements are fundamentally flawed and unsustainable from a Scottish point of view. While many Scottish citizens might agree with this, it is not certain that they think that independence is the only means to enhance and protect Scottish democracy and interests. The SNP is keen to stress that relatively small EU member states such as Ireland and Denmark provide viable examples for Scotland, but a significant number of Scottish citizens might perhaps prefer to look to the examples of non-EU members such as Norway and Iceland. A credible commitment to reform the UK might also fundamentally change the political dynamics surrounding the issue of Scottish independence, although it should perhaps be said that it looks like a rather distant possibility, at least so long as Boris Johnson leads the UK Government. The more consolidated the positions of the Conservative Party in England and the SNP in Scotland become, the less sustainable the current constitutional arrangements of the UK appear. But that, of course, does not necessarily mean that it is easy to envision what would replace it, only that Scotland's place vis-à-vis the UK and Europe will most certainly remain a highly contentious issue for many years to come.

Note

1 This was remarkable since Sillars is usually closely associated with the '79 Group' (together with Alex Salmond among others) and the party's shift in the 1980s towards embracing European integration and EU membership as a prerequisite for Scottish independence (Jackson 2020: 149, 161). As a Labour MP, Sillars had first advocated for a 'no' vote in the UK referendum on EEC membership in 1975 but soon changed his position on the

100   *Scotland*

grounds that there was a qualitative difference to Scottish devolution in the UK after the country had entered the EEC (ibid.; see also Chapter 2 in this volume). Sillars eventually joined the SNP and 'carried these views with him into the SNP in 1980 and continued to develop them in response to the changing character [of European integration]' (ibid.: 150).

References

Biermann, Felix and Jagdhuber, Stefan (2021). Take it and leave it! A post-functionalist bargaining approach to the Brexit negotiations. *West European Politics*, 21 April (online).

Curtice, John (2019). Polarised politics: The European elections in the UK. *Political Insight*, 10 (3), 8–11.

Curtice, John and Montagu, Ian (2020). *Is Brexit fuelling support for independence?* What Scotland Thinks. Available at https://whatscotlandthinks. org/wp-content/uploads/2020/11/SSA-2019-Scotland-paper-v5.pdf (accessed 21 May 2021).

Diamond, Patrick, Nedergaard, Peter and Rosamond, Ben (eds) (2018). *The Routledge handbook of the politics of Brexit*. London: Routledge.

Edward, David (2012) *Scotland and the European Union*. Scottish Constitutional Futures Forum. Available at www.scottishconstitutionalfutures.org/ OpinionandAnalysis/ViewBlogPost/tabid/1767/articleType/ArticleView/artic leId/852/David-Edward-Scotland-and-the-European-Union.aspx (accessed 20 May 2021).

Figueira, Filipa and Martill, Benjamin (2021). Bounded rationality and the Brexit negotiations: Why Britain failed to understand the EU. *Journal of European Public Policy*, 28 (12), 1871–1889.

Hix, Simon (2018). Brexit: Where is the EU–UK relationship heading? *JCMS: Journal of Common Market Studies*, 56 (S1): 11–27.

Jackson, Ben (2020). *The case for Scottish independence: A history of nationalist political thought in modern Scotland*. Cambridge: Cambridge University Press.

Keating, Michael (2001). *Plurinational democracy: Stateless nations in a post-sovereignty era*. Oxford: Oxford University Press.

Keating, Michael (2017). The European question. In Michael Keating (ed.), *Debating Scotland: Issues of independence and union in the 2014 referendum*. Oxford: Oxford University Press.

Keating, Michael and McEwan, Nicola (2017). The Scottish independence debate. In Michael Keating (ed.), *Debating Scotland: Issues of independence and union in the 2014 referendum*. Oxford: Oxford University Press.

Kenealy, Daniel (2014). How do you solve a problem like Scotland? A proposal regarding 'internal enlargement'. *Journal of European Integration*, 36 (6), 585–600.

McTavish, Duncan and Garnett, Mark (2020). Scottish and UK politics: Convergence and divergence. In Mark Garnett (ed.), *The Routledge handbook of British politics and society*. London: Routledge, 244–257.

Scotland 101

Muro, Diego and Vlaskamp, Martijn (2016). How do prospects of EU membership influence support for secession? A survey experiment in Catalonia and Scotland. *West European Politics*, 39 (6), 1115–1138.

Scottish Government (2013a). Scotland's future. *Scottish Government*. Available at www.gov.scot/publications/scotlands-future/ (accessed 20 May 2021).

Scottish Government (2013b). Speech by First Minister Alex Salmond at the Campbeltown Summer Cabinet Public Discussion. *Social Union and the Union of the Crowns*, 28 August. Available at https://scottishgov-newsroom.prgloo.com/speeches-and-briefings/social-union-and-the-union-of-the-crowns (accessed 21 June 2021).

Scottish Government (2016). *Scotland's place in Europe*. Available at www.gov.scot/publications/scotlands-place-europe/ (accessed 20 May 2021).

Scottish Government (2018). *Scotland's place in Europe: Assessment of UK Government's proposed future relationship with the EU*. Available at www.gov.scot/publications/scotlands-place-europe-assessment-uk-governments-proposed-future-relationship-eu/ (accessed 20 May 2021).

Scottish National Party (SNP) (2011). *Scottish election manifesto: Re-elect a Scottish government working for Scotland*.

Scottish National Party (SNP) (2015). *UK election manifesto: Stronger for Scotland*.

Scottish National Party (SNP) (2017). *UK election manifesto: Stronger for Scotland*.

Scottish National Party (SNP) (2019a). *European election manifesto: Scotland's for Europe*.

Scottish National Party (SNP) (2019b). *UK election manifesto: Stronger for Scotland*.

Scottish National Party (SNP) (2020). *We're asking our friends in Europe to leave a light on for Scotland*, 31 January. Available at www.snp.org/we-are-asking-our-friends-in-europe-to-leave-a-light-on-for-scotland/ (accessed 21 May 2021).

Scottish National Party (SNP) (2021). *Scottish election manifesto: Scotland's future*. Available at www.snp.org/manifesto/ (accessed 9 December 2021).

Scothorne, Rory (2021). 'War on woke': The meaning of the Alba Party. *New Statesman*, 1 April. Available at www.newstatesman.com/politics/2021/04/war-woke-meaning-alba-party (accessed 8 December 2021).

Thompson, Helen (2021). How would Scotland work inside the EU? Five years on from Brexit, nationalists still don't have a clue. *New Statesman*, 5 May. Available at www.newstatesman.com/politics/uk/2021/05/how-would-scotland-work-inside-eu-five-years-brexit-nationalists-still-don-t (accessed 20 May 2021).

UK Government (2014). *Scotland analysis: EU and international issues*. Available at www.gov.uk/government/publications/scotland-analysis-eu-and-international-issues (accessed 20 May 2021).

5 Scotland and Catalonia
Comparison and wider implications

The preceding chapters in this volume brought out the distinctive ways in which Europe has featured in the visions and strategies of pro-independence forces in Scotland and Catalonia while also identifying common discursive themes, such as the attractiveness of the idea of 'independence in Europe' and the use of referenda as instruments to pursue a public mandate to press sovereignty claims. In this final chapter, we aim to bring together the preceding individual case studies, clarify the nature of relationships between the parties centrally involved in our comparison, highlight some key thematic areas where we feel that our findings may add to the extant literature on democracy in the EU and the viability of small states in Europe, and consider the significance of this study for the theoretical debates presented in the Introduction.

The Scottish and Catalan cases compared

Comparisons between the Scottish and Catalan nationalist and independence movements have identified various similarities and contrasts between them in terms of their histories, host state contexts, party strategies and forms of political representation. In his historical discussion of the comparison, Elliot makes much of the lack of an earlier Catalan state and brings out some major differences between Scotland and Catalonia in respect of their relationship to their host state, yet he argues that their nationalisms 'converge markedly from the 1970s onwards' following Spain's transition to democracy (2018: 265). Comparative political studies have made rather more reference to the European dimension in which parties seeking independence attempt to further the legitimacy of their goals and find allies. They mainly take the form of case studies rather than sustained comparison, although a notable exception is the work of Jolly, who notes that traditionally

DOI: 10.4324/9781003129028-5

Wider implications of independence in Europe 103

Catalan nationalists (especially Convergència i Unió (CiU), until it was dissolved in 2015) were unreserved Europhiles, whereas the Scottish National Party (SNP) has been more 'instrumental in their support' (2015: 119), a distinction that today needs qualifying in the Catalan case given the more critical tone found in post-CDC political ranks since the referendum in Catalonia in 2017, as well as the EU-hostile stance of the anti-capitalist Candidatura d'Unitat Popular (CUP).

Our contention is that the more instrumental attitude of the SNP towards membership of the European Union (EU) derives not only from concerns about sensitive economic issues such as fishery resources but also from the longstanding focus on sovereignty of a party committed to independence since its foundation in 1934, while operating in a UK that has seen deep controversies over the issue of European Community/EU membership; the party, in common with most other British parties, did not initially welcome the creation of the Community whereas Catalan nationalists, in the form of Esquerra Republicana de Catalunya (ERC), did (see Chapter 2 in this volume). CiU, the largest Catalan nationalist party towards the end of the twentieth century, sought enhanced autonomy within Spain, potentially progressing to some form of shared sovereignty, in a region and a state that were very broadly pro-European. A majority of Catalans went on to demonstrate their acceptance of compromise within the Spanish context by voting in favour of a reform of their autonomy statute in 2006, only to see this critically diluted by Spain's Constitutional Court in 2010. Catalan sovereignty-seeking parties remained strongly committed to deeper European integration, with none of the reservations such as those held by the SNP about the Common Fisheries Policy.

A more interactive dynamic in relations between EU elites and Catalan nationalist parties began to emerge during the debates on a European Constitution in the early 2000s, used by the Generalitat de Catalunya (Government of Catalonia) as an opportunity to involve sectors of civil society in articulating demands for a more decentralized Europe in which the languages of the smaller nations might feature more prominently in the workings of EU institutions. Their proposals being ignored by EU leaders, notwithstanding the prominent role played by Catalans within the organization, many Catalanists who sought greater fulfilment in Europe began to see a need to establish some form of state of their own, since it was now evident that the member states were going to continue to dominate EU decision-making. The main driver behind the growing desire for Catalonia to take its own decisions, however, continued to reside in the tension

104 *Wider implications of independence in Europe*

within Spain that began to take on the dimensions of a conflict through the failure of the attempt to reform the statute of autonomy.

The last decade has seen a new challenge for the EU, since a union hitherto characterized by periodic enlargements and now facing increasing problems of coordination as the number of member states has grown, has been asked to consider 'internal enlargement' under pressure from both legal and illegal referenda on independence in some of its larger member states. This has been an unwelcome development for a union that has been seeking to assert itself as a global actor and already possesses the disadvantage of having 'by far the highest ratio of separate political units to surface area' among global actors (Howorth, 2010: 458). In many ways, initially, the SNP's ambitions were easier for the EU, the UK and Scots to consider. Despite having independence as a goal from an earlier date than the main parties of Catalan nationalism, by the time it came onto the agenda as a possible outcome of the referendum of 2014 the SNP had a vision of Scotland becoming a European state while retaining several aspects of its union with the rest of the UK, including the sterling-based currency union. The Edinburgh Agreement enabled it to pursue independence through democratic channels, thus avoiding a strong EU response, even if policymakers in Brussels regretted the precedent that was being set.

In Catalonia, a different constitutional context and the unsympathetic response of the Rajoy Government in Madrid, refusing to negotiate politically or allow even a consultative referendum, made the EU potentially a more critically important actor in a scene of growing confrontation, as illegal referendums proceeded to take place in 2014 and 2017. Senior EU officials effectively upheld the position of the Spanish Government, but the eventual crackdown on the independence movement gave it opportunities to take its calls for an international response to a wider European audience – within and beyond the EU itself – and to raise issues about fundamental European values and rights. Although the EU official position of non-involvement in the internal affairs of a member state remained unchanged, even among European Commission leaders there was quiet encouragement of a more conciliatory attitude in Madrid and tacit support was apparent when the Sánchez Government finally agreed to a dialogue with its Catalan counterpart and went on to pardon independence leaders in June 2021, by which time Spain was under more public pressure from the Council of Europe, both to take such steps and to go further by dropping extradition requests against independence politicians living abroad.

Wider implications of independence in Europe 105

Although Catalan independence leaders have experienced a series of rebuffs in Europe, chiefly from the European Commission and within the European Parliament (EP), our analysis leads us to conclude that in both the Scottish and Catalan cases there has been quite an effective deployment of 'Europe' on the part of pro-independence parties. Not only have they used it successfully to reassure their compatriots that there is a potential alternative to forming part of a larger country: they have also gained some ground through their political activities in Europe to counter the official EU line that those demanding referendums are secessionists whose success would lead to a weaker Europe. To some extent they have managed to counter the negativity that many associate with secessionism, insisting that their project is not secessionist but rather is about reconfiguring and increasing their nation's participation in Europe. The separatist label is contested too by presenting their movements as essentially democratic in that they want their national communities to be able to vote on the question of independence, which their host state has tried to block, continually in Spain and post-Brexit in the UK. In addition, the SNP has been able to present a powerful argument about a majority in Scotland having voted to remain in the EU whereas the UK majority opted to leave the Union. Notwithstanding the nationalist roots of the major Catalan and Scottish parties, public support has been built by advancing democratic demands for self-government in old nations where many citizens today feel more confident about finding a new, more autonomous future both within and through the EU.

Despite receiving only minority support in the referendums held thus far, partial gains in levels of public support have owed much to party efforts to internationalize independence causes, largely through action in Europe. Yet while Europeanization strategies have had a degree of effectiveness, this is not to say that the protagonists are necessarily on their way to successful bids for independence. The much more sympathetic treatment of SNP representatives in Europe since 2016 is far more a consequence of Brexit, which the party opposed, than it is of the SNP's commitment to acting legally and constitutionally. The UK's withdrawal from the EU left pro-European Scotland feeling unrepresented by the government in Westminster and greatly boosted the SNP's position in electoral terms, allowing it to make the case for a second referendum in the coming years. Typically, for this party, it has spoken of making an appeal to the UK Supreme Court, rather than unilateral political mobilization, if the Johnson Government or its successor continues to refuse to negotiate.

However, British secession from the EU has transformed the debate over Scottish independence in that the half-way house proposed in

106 *Wider implications of independence in Europe*

2014 is no longer available and in a second referendum on independence Scots would be faced with a choice between two unions, the EU or the UK: these being much starker alternatives than those that were on offer on the first occasion. They would need to contemplate EU expectations that a new Scottish member state would join the euro (BBC 15 September 2019) and face the prospect of a border being created between Scotland and the rest of the UK. 'Independence in Europe' has become a more complex, less certain, issue than it appeared to be in 2014. While the SNP, post-Brexit, has received hospitable treatment on the part of EU leaders, it is now in a weaker position to negotiate accession on its own terms. While pro-Europeans have rallied around the party in greater numbers, the current debate about the possible downsides of EU accession for Scotland may be leading some traditional party voters to waver in their desire for independence.

In Catalonia, meanwhile, pro-independence parties have been able to attract sympathy in Europe, initially through pleading their cause via massive, imaginatively organized and well publicized mobilizations of public support and then by proceeding peaceably to defy Spanish bans on unconstitutional activity. Thereafter they were able to exploit the use of a huge police operation by the Rajoy Government to try to prevent voting in October 2017 and the subsequent prosecution of actors deemed responsible for that event. Notwithstanding considerable consistency in official EU positions, the shift from purely negative to more varied European responses to Catalan independence demands has been encouraging to activists, as have the positive vibes emanating from the EU on Scotland, which some Catalans have taken as a sign that independence in Europe may still be possible for Catalonia, should a firm majority there be convinced by that idea and if some way can be found to legally negotiate a referendum allowing for that outcome. The former President of the European Council, Herman Van Rompuy, confirmed that there was not only greater EU positivity on Scottish independence but also 'much more sympathy' for European regions seeking independence (Van Rompuy 2019).

However, when Spain's dialogue with Catalonia really got underway, in 2021, Sánchez's Government quickly ruled out the possibility of authorizing a Catalan referendum or declaring an amnesty. While his administration was willing to reach agreements with the Catalan Government on other matters, it knew that the increased differences among the independence parties post-2017 meant that the threat of separation had become, for the present at least, easier to counter. In Sánchez's view, the task was not to resolve the Catalan conflict, which

Wider implications of independence in Europe 107

(in agreement with Ortega y Gasset in the 1930s) he felt was simply not possible, so much as to manage an enduring tension, by pardoning independence leaders, offering Catalans a better economic deal and devolving further powers to the Generalitat (*El País* 5 July, 24 July 2021). While this was something that ERC was willing to discuss, while still demanding self-determination and an amnesty, more radical sectors found the offer inadequate and, in any case, unfeasible, for in their opinion either the judiciary or a general election resulting in a right-wing Partido Popular-Vox coalition would get in the way of any substantial political concessions.

Cross-fertilization in the EU between Scottish and Catalan pro-independence parties

Ask leading figures in the Catalan or Scottish pro-independence parties whether they regard any other independence movement as a model, relevant to the pursuit of their own objectives, and they are likely to play down the suggestion. While acknowledging the deep interest of their party in other independence 'processes', they will tend to emphasize the distinctiveness of their domestic context and perhaps also point to differences in 'rhythm', relating to the rough timescales they envisage for the potential achievement of independence in each country. While sometimes reflecting claims to uniqueness in nationalist political outlooks and more generally a recognition that the specific causes behind the strengthening of pro-independence feeling are indeed different from case to case (Puigdemont interview 2013), there may be also an element of cautiousness here, arising from concerns that direct identification of their own national movement with another would be a hostage to fortune, with any setbacks for the other movement potentially damaging morale within their own ranks and being seized upon by political opponents to undermine their own movement's credibility and legitimacy. Equally (although only pre-Brexit in the case of Catalonia), the desire of pro-independence parties to accede to the EU once statehood has been achieved may temper any overt identification with other European cases where territorial separation might occur, in order to avoid giving member states that would be weakened thereby a defensible reason to veto accession. Independence parties in the EU consider not only what they have in common with counterparts but also how their international activity will impact politically on other member states in the event of themselves achieving statehood.

In response to the questions about change and continuity raised in Chapter 2 in this volume it is worth noticing that while Catalan pro-

108 *Wider implications of independence in Europe*

independence activists frequently refer to Scotland in their arguments, partly because they know that its status within the UK allows the SNP agenda to appear comparatively more legitimate in Europe (Strubell interview 2014), Scottish nationalist discourses refer less frequently to Catalonia. Operating within the legal and constitutional framework of the UK, the SNP has been emphatic that the Catalan case, involving a resort to illegal referenda, a cavalier attitude towards established parliamentary procedures and defiance of court injunctions, is different to the circumstances of Scotland. As Raphael Minder noted, 'nationalist movements that do quite well tend to dissociate themselves from the others' (2017: 148).

Yet while there has never been an attempt to create an international alliance composed of such parties, there are significant interactions between the Scottish and Catalan independence movements and these have grown over the last decade as both have acquired the capacity to place the holding of referenda on the political agenda. Observation of party and civil society international activity reveals considerable empathy between them, above and beyond more instrumental reasons for cooperation and solidarity. The reality is one of mutual sympathy but not of unqualified solidarity, for expressions of solidarity at the most senior levels are 'ultimately contingent on how expressions of solidarity might serve (or counteract) domestic goals' (Sijstermans and Brown Swan 2021a). Within parties, feelings of solidarity are stronger at the grassroots level and this can put pressure on party leaders to be more forthright at key junctures in the independence challenge (Sijstermans and Brown Swan 2021b: 8).

Over several decades, both Catalan and Scottish nationalist and pro-independence parties have taken part in European institutions to further their domestic political interests and demonstrate to domestic audiences that they are legitimate political actors (Laible 2008: 153). In office in 1980–2003 and 2010–2015, CiU enjoyed many uninterrupted years of opportunity to engage in paradiplomacy in Europe, as too have pro-independence coalitions during the past decade. Repeated electoral triumphs for the SNP since 2011 have also generated opportunities to collaborate internationally, but these have not been used exclusively to build regionally based party alliances. Indeed, when the party first had an MEP elected in 1979, the SNP shared the federated CiU parties' proclivity to operate within mainstream groups in the EP rather than join the much weaker grouping of regionally based nationalist parties, the European Free Alliance (EFA), although subsequently the Scots' involvement with EFA parties grew both in the EP and through the Committee of the Regions (CoR) (Lynch

Wider implications of independence in Europe 109

2006: 248). Neither CDC nor UDC joined the Alliance, whereas ERC did, albeit while still a relatively marginal force in Catalan politics, and the EFA would later be outspoken in condemning the imprisonment of Oriol Junqueras and other Catalan independence leaders.

There were certainly bilateral consultations between the Scottish and Catalan Governments ahead of the referenda in 2014, partly to discuss sequencing. Although apparently at one point both executives thought it best if the Catalan consultation were to precede the Scottish event by a few days, it ultimately made more sense for the second Mas administration to use Scotland's vote in September as a backdrop to the Catalan consultation in November and for the Scottish referendum not to be affected by the illegality of the event in Catalonia (Bosch interview 2013; Gardner 2012). The Edinburgh Agreement made the UK/Scottish example a key international point of reference for the second Mas Government and for pro-referendum and *independentista* forces in Catalonia. UK Prime Minister David Cameron's explanation as to why he had agreed to a Scottish referendum was read out by an Iniciativa per Catalunya Verds deputy in the Catalan Parliament and was described by an ERC deputy as 'absolutely marvellous, very brave' (Amorós interview 2014). With Rajoy refusing to authorize a referendum in Catalonia, pro-independence activists there and in Scotland were each telling the other how lucky they were in terms of their adversary: the Catalans because Cameron had negotiated a roadmap leading to a legal referendum and the Scots because Rajoy's intransigent attitude was driving those Catalans just wanting enhanced self-government into the secessionist camp, thus making an overall majority for independence more likely. Cameron and Rajoy themselves met in Vilnius, Lithuania, in November 2013 to discuss the independence challenges. While viewing them very differently, they agreed that they would both warn about exclusion from the EU in the event of separation (*El País* 29 November 2013).

Around this time, the difference between the two cases was emphasized too by the SNP leader, Alex Salmond, hoping for eventual Spanish support in Europe in the event of Scottish independence (Duerr 2015: 109). In contrast, the UK example was central to the case made by the Mas administration when seeking permission to hold a referendum. It presented a 'law on consultations' to the Catalan Parliament on 19 September 2014, one day after the Scottish referendum, which Mas lauded for its 'normality', implying that this was the correct way to behave in a democracy. Meanwhile, Mariano Rajoy invoked the case of Crimea in warning against secessionism in Catalonia.

110 *Wider implications of independence in Europe*

In terms of bilateral solidarity, the Catalans continued to make most of the running in the years that followed, while the SNP, at the executive level, remained more measured in their expressions of solidarity. These were less intense and cohesive than those of the Flemish nationalists of the Nieuw-Vlaamse Alliantie. The latter welcomed Carles Puigdemont to Belgium in 2017 and Flemish Prime Minister Geert Bourgeois made an official visit to Catalonia after Quim Torra i Pla took office in 2018 (Sijstermans and Brown Swan 2021b: 14–15). Under both Salmond and Sturgeon successively, the SNP defended the right of Catalans to vote in a referendum, but it distanced itself from unilateralism. In the aftermath of the UK's Brexit referendum of June 2016, Salmond (now SNP spokesperson for international affairs and Europe at Westminster) urged the Catalan pro-independence forces to continue to seek permission for a referendum since the Spanish Government's position could change. However, he insisted that the Scottish situation could not be translated to Catalonia given that Spain was not interested in leaving the EU. The warm welcome given to Nicola Sturgeon in Brussels by Jean-Claude Juncker and Martin Schulz after the British referendum made the differences clearer in terms of the European context. While refusing to meet Puigdemont, Juncker said that Scotland had a right to be listened to in Brussels (*El Periódico de Catalunya* 30 June 2016).

Typical of the balancing act performed by Sturgeon was her declaration in the Scottish Parliament, ten days before the Catalan referendum of 2017, when she argued that it was 'entirely legitimate' for Spain to oppose independence for Catalonia while saying it was 'a concern if any state seeks to deny people's right to democratically express their will', thus upholding the general principle of self-determination (Sjisterman and Brown Swan 2021b: 8). While EU leaders were prepared to consider the balanced, measured statements of Sturgeon, she herself was now coming under pressure from the ranks of her party to become more supportive as the Catalan movement's bid for independence reached a peak. Tensions within the SNP were evident at its annual conference in October, coming just days after the Catalan Parliament's declaration in favour of Catalonia becoming an independent republic. Many SNP activists and some 21 SNP members of the Scottish Parliament (one-third of the parliamentary group) urged this to be recognized, but the conference only voted for the declaration to be 'respected'. Not wanting to antagonize Madrid and in view of its own ambition to secure another legally secure vote on independence based on something similar to the Edinburgh Agreement, the party executive thus secured an outcome that allowed it to

Wider implications of independence in Europe 111

remain silent on the declaration (BBC 2017; *Político* 3 November 2017). Nevertheless, the mood of the conference was supportive and Sturgeon herself made reference to the police violence in Spain. Representatives of the Catalan Government were present, there were lots of Catalan flags and the BBC reported 'vast sympathy amid the SNP's activist base for the Catalans'. There was a strong feeling that the EU should have done more to question Madrid's management of the Catalan challenge and even mediate in the conflict, although this did not affect the party's commitment to EU membership (BBC 2017). Those demanding more fulsome solidarity were told that the Government did not want to set a precedent for other governments to interfere with Scottish independence (*The Guardian* 12 July 2018).

SNP ministers were clearly more comfortable with expressing solidarity with the Catalan movement in response to its 'repression' than in positioning themselves politically on the conflict. Advocacy of a democratic approach to its resolution, upholding a rights agenda without giving specific political support, allowed them to maintain some distance from a Catalan movement, part of which remained unilateralist and urged 'disobedience' to the state. In one respect, this approach seemed to be paying off once the Partido Socialista Obrero Español had returned to office under Pedro Sánchez Pérez-Castejón. In November 2018, Minister of Foreign Affairs Josep Borrell announced that Spain would not oppose the inclusion of an independent Scotland in the EU, so long as it left the UK in accordance with the laws of the country – a statement hailed by the SNP as a historic change of course by Spain (*El País* 21 November 2018). This did not prevent Sturgeon from tweeting her condemnation of the long sentences issued by the Supreme Court in the trial of the Catalan leaders as a 'dreadful outcome' or asking in her October 2018 SNP conference address for support and solidarity with them, in the knowledge that many in Europe saw the sentences as unjust and the Catalan independence challenge as requiring a political response from Spain.

Somewhat ironically, the 'judicialization' of Spanish policy on Catalonia (as some described Rajoy's decision to deal with the Catalan challenge through the courts) eventually brought Scotland more directly into the international battle that was fought over Catalan *independentista* activity in Europe following the clampdown on the movement in Spain. The Catalan ministers who fled to Brussels, Belgium, to avoid imprisonment included former Minister of Education Clara Ponsatí, an economist who earlier had headed the School of Economics and Finance at the University of St Andrews in Scotland. In March 2018, after a Spanish judge had temporarily dropped the

112 *Wider implications of independence in Europe*

international and European arrest warrants he had issued against her, she announced that she had returned to Scotland to resume her academic career. Further Spanish attempts to extradite her ran into difficulties in the Scottish courts and led to a serious setback in March 2020 when Edinburgh Sheriff Court ruled that, in her capacity as an MEP (following post-Brexit EP seat adjustments), she enjoyed immunity (which the EP proceeded to remove a year later). Ponsatí's presence in Scotland became a rallying point for SNP activists wanting to show more fulsome political support for the Catalan independence movement.

The Scottish executive's caution over its relations with the Generalitat was seen, too, when it came to high-level visits. While individual SNP activists went to Catalonia to support the referendum campaign in 2017, there were no visits by party leaders. Nor were there any invitations to presidents of the Generalitat to visit Scotland officially, although Puigdemont travelled there from Brussels in August 2018 to give a talk and Torra was received by Sturgeon the previous month, at the request of the Catalan Government; he used the opportunity to express admiration for the 'Scottish model' and referred to the Scottish referendum as 'an example for the world' (*The Independent* 5 July 2018; *The Guardian* 12 July 2018). The minutes of the meeting indicated agreement between the leaders on the need for a democratic and peaceful solution in Catalonia, involving dialogue between the regional and Spanish authorities and respecting the right to self-determination (BBC 21 August 2018). In fact, Torra remained sceptical about the possibility of a meaningful dialogue with Madrid, unconvinced by ERC's efforts to make it happen.

Since the events of 2017, publicly aired differences between Junts per Catalunya (JxCat) and ERC over the means of pursuing independence and the value of dialogue with the Sánchez Government have left the SNP still more cautious about relations with the Generalitat, where increasingly deep divisions between the coalition parties found public expression both prior to the Catalan election in February 2021 and in the difficulty experienced in negotiating a new coalition agreement after ERC emerged with greater electoral support than JxCat. Strangely, following the SNP's victory in the Scottish elections in May, it was the anti-EU CUP that now began to speak of the need to synchronize calendars with the Scottish people with the aim of bringing about a debate on the right to self-determination at the European level; its readiness to compromise was strengthened by concern that collaboration between the pro-independence parties might break down completely. A breakthrough was reached finally in May when, based

Wider implications of independence in Europe 113

on separate ERC agreements with the CUP and JxCat, an ERC-JxCat coalition was formed under Pere Aragonès i Garcia. During the investiture session in the Catalan Parliament, ERC's first Catalan President of the Generalitat since the 1930s said that he wanted Catalonia to be like Scotland and Spain to be like the UK; he confidently expected a second Scottish referendum, although this was being refused by Boris Johnson. Aragonès committed himself to the pursuit of a negotiated referendum through a combination of 'civic, peaceful confrontation' and dialogue with the Spanish Government, yet an authorized referendum on independence still seemed a remote prospect. It was a sign of the new Catalan Government's weakness that, in return for JxCat and CUP support, the new Catalan President had needed to concede that this strategy would be reviewed within two years. And it was a sign of ongoing division that ERC leader Junqueras proceeded to describe unilateralism, even as a fallback, as being neither 'desirable nor viable', while JxCat and the CUP continued to defend it (*El País* 10, 20–21 May, 7 June 2021).

The contested meaning of 'Europe' in Scotland and Catalonia

The analytical framework that has guided our study of Scottish and Catalan pro-independence parties and the development of the secessionist challenge over time in these two cases combines insights from post-functionalism, constructivism and studies on the politics of everyday Europe (see Chapter 1 in this volume). The framework has allowed us to analyse visions and strategies of these parties with a particular emphasis on the ways in which notions of 'Europe', the EU and European integration are used and made to resonate with their independence claims. The findings from our study indicate that parties such as the SNP in Scotland and ERC in Catalonia frequently deploy visions of Scottish and Catalan independence that are presented as deeply connected to the ideal of European integration and the norms and values of the EU. This is in keeping with what we would expect based on previous studies suggesting that one of the main effects of European integration and EU membership on party strategies is that small states are perceived to be more viable since independence can be sought within a common European framework for economic and political cooperation (Cram 2009; Laible 2008; Jolly 2007).

However, our study also shows that the meaning of 'Europe' is being increasingly contested by some pro-independence parties in Catalonia. This is related to the perceived lack of support from EU leaders in the aftermath of the unconstitutional Catalan 'referendum'

114 *Wider implications of independence in Europe*

on independence in 2017. As noted above, the shift is most noticeable among post-CDC political ranks, while the anti-capitalist CUP has taken a critical stance towards the EU for a much longer time. But that a political leader such as Carles Puigdemont is publicly criticizing the EU for, in his view, failing to live up to the Union's own ideals and values, needs not only to be understood as an instrumental use of 'Europe' for short-term political gain since it has to resonate somehow with people's expectations and ideas of what it means to be a citizen of an EU member state today.

Thus, the struggle over how to frame Catalan independence and how to relate such claims to the process of European integration reveal certain taken-for-granted notions about what living in the EU should entail. Whether or not to further exploit certain Catalans' sense of disappointment with the EU is of course a political choice, but from the perspective of our analytical framework the possibility of a shared sense of disappointment among pro-independence supporters is of interest as it would suggest that people might actually consider themselves as belonging to a political community that is at the same time smaller (Catalonia) and bigger (the EU) than the host state (Spain), and that this is to a large extent a function of EU membership.

The findings from our study of the Scottish case and the evolution of SNP party discourse also contribute to advance our knowledge of the uses of 'Europe' to make independence claims appear legitimate. Beyond the well-established trope in SNP discourse that an independent Scotland would be able to better promote Scottish interests in Europe as a full member of the EU, Brexit has offered the SNP an opportunity to broaden its discursive repertoire. Pursuing independence is presented as a means for Scotland to rejoin the EU. Interestingly, EU membership is presented as something that 'normal' European countries hold or aspire to, at least the ones with which the SNP wants to express political and ideological affinity, such as Ireland, Denmark and Sweden. As such, the notion of belonging to 'Europe' becomes a device for the SNP to further distance Scotland from the rest of the UK, particularly England, in the post-Brexit setting. This is based not only on the fact that Scottish voters voted to remain in the EU but also by way of emphasizing that the British Conservatives' vision of the UK outside of the EU is utterly harmful to Scottish interests.

But our analysis has also highlighted that the notion of belonging to 'Europe', and thus strongly linking Scottish independence and EU membership together, might not be unproblematic since membership

Wider implications of independence in Europe 115

of the EU nowadays entails making tough political choices for Scotland, not least in relation to border issues. Opinion data also suggest that Scottish citizens are perhaps not overwhelmingly enthusiastic about the EU, even though many are deeply dissatisfied with Brexit. This, in combination with the fact that there are several examples of well-functioning Northern European countries that are not members of the EU (Norway and Iceland), seems to suggest that the meaning of belonging to 'Europe' could become increasingly contested in Scotland in the years ahead, if political actors in Scotland and the UK manage to articulate alternative visions on independence and integration.

Another important finding from our study is that the notion of democracy is deeply connected not only to claims of independence but also visions of European integration in the discourses of pro-independence parties in Catalonia and Scotland. In our view, this indicates that increasing contestation around European integration is not only a function of exclusive national identities and elite strategies, as post-functionalism suggests (Hooghe and Marks 2009), but that understandings of the normative and democratic foundations of the EU's political order also play a significant part in these political dynamics. In Scotland and Catalonia, pro-independence parties are presenting their claims as based on a basic democratic ideal, namely that people should be allowed to have a meaningful say about how they want to be governed. This does not entail that there is an undisputable legal right to self-determination for stateless nations. It is more of a moral case that the pro-independence parties are presenting. The fact that some are willing to negotiate with the host state implies that there are other interested parties' rights to be considered too. But what is relevant to note in the view of our analytical framework is that although these independence claims are directed towards the national governments in London and Madrid, as they are the main interlocutors for the Scottish and Catalan Governments, they can also be said to be addressing all democratic countries in Europe, its citizens as well as EU institutions.

It is not hard to understand why other EU member states and the European Commission are very reluctant to express support for Scottish and Catalan independence, or even support popular referendums as a way to move the issue forward, but we nonetheless think that the role that appeals to democratic ideals play in the parties' visions and strategies provides an opportunity to contribute to ongoing debates on EU democracy. These debates have in many ways moved beyond earlier discussions on whether or not there is a 'democratic deficit' in the

116 *Wider implications of independence in Europe*

EU (see Chapter 1 in this volume), to address in more nuanced ways a broader range of issues and problems that more or less explicitly acknowledge that there are inherent trade-offs and dilemmas involved in any attempts to further democratize policymaking in a multilevel governance system like the EU (Bremberg and Norman forthcoming).

Of particular relevance for the question of how regional secessionism in European states relates to questions about democracy in the EU and European integration is the debate around the notion of 'demoicracy' (Bellamy 2013; Cheneval and Schimmelfennig 2013; Cheneval and Nicolaidis 2017). This notion departs from the assertion that there is no common European *demos* but rather a multitude of different *demoi* in Europe. To be democratically legitimate, the powers and competences of the EU therefore need to be designed and exercised so that the peoples of the EU can govern themselves together within a common European framework, but not necessarily govern as *one* people. This understanding of democracy in the EU is often portrayed by its advocates as an alternative to supranational democracy in the EU and European federalism as well as the disintegration of the EU, as neither option is deemed feasible or desirable.

Fabio Wolkenstein (2018: 286) has noted that many proponents of 'demoicracy' in the EU adhere to republican ideals in which power, to be exercised legitimately, must be responsive to those 'who regard themselves as a political community that is capable of self-government'. But a community that would not regard itself as capable of self-rule in some form or another would simply not be a *political* community. This is a fundamental constructivist insight upon which our framework draws, and it acknowledges that any notion of self-determination ultimately rests on a tautological claim. The claim basically consists of an assertion of ability to govern, made on behalf of a group of people, because the group exists as a social fact and therefore has a right to self-determination (Keating et al. 2019). However, in our view the relevant point to make here is that there is not only a multitude of *demoi* in Europe with regards to the powers and competences of the EU, but also in relation to many of its member states. Many pro-independence parties and their supporters in Scotland and Catalonia argue that Scotland and Catalonia are political communities entitled to self-government, and that they are already in fact governing themselves, to a certain extent, within a common European framework due to the combination of European integration and decentralization in their host states. In practice, Spain has gone some way towards recognizing this fact by designating its constituent regions as 'autonomous communities', but without

Wider implications of independence in Europe 117

differentiating between the constitutional status of politico-geographical areas and areas that are home to stateless nations.

To be sure, the sense that independence claims are based on democratic ideals that should be respected across all democratic states in Europe is what is increasingly defining the struggle over the meaning of independence and integration in our two cases. It is thus something that needs to be further addressed both in empirical studies that seek to measure and explain what factors shape public opinion and elite strategies vis-à-vis the EU and EU policymaking, as well as work in political theory that seeks to advance our understanding of the moral and normative basis of the power and competences of the EU and democratic governance beyond the state. Although we are not arguing that our study necessarily provides a basis for recommendations as to how the conflict in Catalonia or the dispute over Scotland's future could be resolved, we do think that it has a contribution to make to thinking about the role of regions and secessionism in contemporary Europe.

Regional secessionism as a democratic challenge to the political order in the EU

We would like to conclude this chapter by suggesting that the democratic challenge to the current political order in the EU arises as soon as individuals who feel that they belong to Scotland and Catalonia as members of distinct political communities also feel that their right to self-determination is not satisfactorily expressed within the constitutional arrangement in which they currently find themselves. Thus, while responding to Catalan claims for a referendum on independence by way of arguing that it can never be considered because secession is unconstitutional according to the Spanish Constitution might make perfect sense from a legalistic point of view, it is clearly a circular argument in political terms that only seems to exacerbate the problem. Similarly, arguing that Scottish citizens had their chance to vote for independence in 2014 and that people only get to vote on such important matters 'once in a generation', as the current UK Government does, appears arbitrary at best and frivolous at worst, and hardly provides for a serious debate on Scotland's future post-Brexit.

We are not arguing that the perceived right to self-determination that members of a given political community might feel is in itself enough to justify unconstitutional actions of secession in the EU. In representative democracies based on effective electoral competition it is fundamental that political actors respect the principles of the rule of

118 *Wider implications of independence in Europe*

law. The lessons from European history also suggest that state borders should only change as a result of negotiated agreements, not by force. But at the same time it is important to acknowledge that there is an inherent tension in all liberal democracies between the need to respect the principles of the rule of law and the need to ensure that popular demands are politically expressed and that those demands that do find broad popular support have a chance to meaningfully influence policymaking, as long as fundamental rights are upheld. This tension might contribute to the dynamic evolution of politics in liberal democratic countries if political actors creatively find ways to accommodate diverging claims, but it can also lead to protracted conflicts and political stalemates which might threaten the stability of the country and its political system, as well as its international reputation. Denying that this tension exists at all is often part of the problem, whereas the example of the Canadian Clarity Act of 1998 (see Chapter 1 in this volume) suggests that there are some ways to handle it that may be more tactful than others.

While our study suggests that there is an enduring and possibly growing appeal for self-determination in Scotland and Catalonia, it seems not primarily to be fuelled by nationalist sentiments, even if they certainly exist as well. A large part of the explanation for the electoral success of Scottish and Catalan pro-independence parties in recent decades seems instead to rest on a growing sense of disillusion and weariness among voters vis-à-vis established state structures in the UK and Spain. This is perhaps not unique to these states, but the increasing contestation and politicization around issues of sovereignty and representation have found a particular political expression there due to the history of British and Spanish state-building and collective experiences of democratic rule (Elliot 2018; Keating 2021). However, we believe that it is important to acknowledge that if the appeal for self-determination partly rests on citizens in Scotland and Catalonia not being satisfied with the quality of democracy in their host states, then independence might actually be offered as a solution to a problem it cannot really solve. In the context of European integration, the question to ask should perhaps rather be how autonomous regions could contribute to strengthen democratic governance in the EU's multilevel system, of which its member states are a fundamental part.

For instance, the CoR of the EU serves today as an advisory body representing local and regional authorities. It is not a political body in which autonomous regions are exclusively represented in the decision-making processes of the EU. Based on our study, we believe that there is room for further debate on how regions with a comparatively high

Wider implications of independence in Europe 119

level of political autonomy and democratic institutions, such as regional parliaments, should be allowed greater influence over issues in the EU that directly concern them, such as regional funds, public procurement and investments, transnational infrastructure and transport networks. The European Commission could decide to reconsider the role of European regions with the purpose of advancing the debate on how democratic governance in the EU, its member states and interested non-members could be improved. This kind of initiative might possibly spur more detailed, engaged and practical debates among citizens, national politicians, EU officials and experts.

One must recognize, however, that the potential for EU actors to play a useful role has been affected somewhat by Brexit, in that the UK is one of few European states where the central government is most immediately challenged by pro-independence parties in office at the regional level. There is thus clearly a need for further debate additionally in states that have unitary traditions, including the UK as well as Spain, about different constitutional formulas that might provide a way of reducing existing tensions, strengthening self-government and reconfiguring relationships between institutions while maintaining collaboration in fields where there is mutual interest in so doing. In Spain itself, the challenge is especially complex since, beyond the question of reform of political institutions and relationships, the case will be made for greater cultural recognition of Catalonia's distinctiveness and for its language to play a bigger role in the EU: an issue on which Spain itself currently has a large say.

Finally, we think that there is much to be gained by adhering to Michael Keating's (2019: 321) suggestion that self-determination in contemporary Europe should be seen as 'a matter of political practice and accommodation of competing claims' rather than a choice between binary choices in relation to independence. To be sure, debates on secessionism in relation to European states would most certainly advance if the secessionist challenge were to be understood as an opportunity to start discussing how to further strengthen democracy and the sense of community among peoples and citizens in Europe by way of asking them to reflect on what kind of political community the EU, its member states and their neighbours should strive to build in the 21st century.

References

Barberà, Òscar and Barrio, Astrid (2006). Convergència i Unió: From stability to decline? In Lieven De Winter, Margarita Gómez-Reino and Peter Lynch

120 *Wider implications of independence in Europe*

(eds), *Autonomist parties in Europe: Identity politics and the revival of the territorial cleavage.* Vol. 1. Barcelona: Institut de Ciències Polítiques i Socials.

Bellamy, Richard (2013). 'An ever closer union among the peoples of Europe': Republican intergovernmentalism and demoicratic representation within the EU. *Journal of European Integration*, 35 (5): 499–516.

Bremberg, Niklas and Norman, Ludvig (eds) (forthcoming). *Democratic dilemmas of Europe's political order.* Edinburgh: Edinburgh University Press.

British Broadcasting Corporation (BBC) (2017). *SNP conference: What did we learn?* 10 October.

Cheneval, Francis and Nicolaidis, Kalypso (2017). The social construction of demoicracy in the European Union. *European Journal of Political Theory*, 16 (2): 235–260.

Cheneval, Francis and Schimmelfennig, Frank (2013). The case for demoicracy in the European Union. *JCMS: Journal of Common Market Studies*, 51 (2): 334–350.

Cram, Laura (2009). Introduction: Banal Europeanism: European Union identity and national identities in synergy. *Nations and Nationalism*, 15 (1): 101–108.

De Winter, Lieven, Gómez-Reino, Margarita and Lynch, Peter (eds) (2006). *Autonomist parties in Europe: Identity politics and the revival of the territorial cleavage.* Vol. 1. Barcelona: Institut de Ciències Polítiques i Socials.

Duerr, Glen M. E. (2015). *Secessionism and the European Union: The future of Flanders, Scotland and Catalonia.* Lanham, MD: Lexington Books.

Elliot, John H. (2018). *Scots and Catalans: Union and disunion.* New Haven, CT: Yale University Press.

Gardner, David (2012). Catalonia looks to Scots for inspiration. *Financial Times*, 25 October.

Hooghe, Liesbet and Marks, Gary (2009). A postfunctionalist theory of European integration: From permissive consensus to constraining dissensus. *British Journal of Political Science*, 39 (1): 1–23.

Howorth, Jolyon (2010). The EU as a global actor: Grand strategy for a global grand bargain? *JCMS: Journal of Common Market Studies*, 48 (3): 455–474.

Jolly, Seth K. (2007). The Europhile fringe? Regionalist party support for European integration. *European Union Politics*, 8 (1): 109–130.

Jolly, Seth K. (2015). *The European Union and the rise of nationalist parties.* Ann Arbor: University of Michigan Press.

Keating, Michael (2019). Is a theory of self-determination possible? *Ethnopolitics*, 18 (3): 315–323.

Keating, Michael (2021). *State and nation in the United Kingdom: The fractured union.* Oxford: Oxford University Press.

Keating, Michael, Jordana, Jacint, Marx, Axel and Wouters, Jan (2019). States, sovereignty, borders, self-determination in Europe. In Jacint

Wider implications of independence in Europe 121

Jordana, Michael Keating, Axel Marx and Jan Wouters (eds), *Changing borders in Europe: Exploring the dynamics of integration, differentiation and self-determination in the European Union*. London: Routledge.

Lynch, Peter (2006). The Scottish National Party: The long road from marginality to blackmail and coalition potential. In Lieven De Winter, Margarita Gómez-Reino and Peter Lynch (eds), *Autonomist parties in Europe: Identity politics and the revival of the territorial cleavage*. Vol. 1. Barcelona: Institut de Ciències Polítiques i Socials.

Laible, Janet (2008). *Separatism and sovereignty in the new Europe: Party politics and the meanings of statehood in a supranational context*. New York: Palgrave Macmillan.

Minder, Raphael (2017). *The struggle for Catalonia*. London: Hurst.

Sijstermans, Judith and Brown Swan, Coree (2021a). *Shades of solidarity: Comparing Scottish and Flemish responses to Catalonia*. University of Edinburgh, Centre on Constitutional Change, 10 February. Available at www.centreonconstitutionalchange.ac.uk/news-and-opinion/shades-solidarit y-comparing-scottish-and-flemish-responses-catalan-referendum (accessed 25 August 2021).

Sijstermans, Judith and Brown Swan, Coree (2021b). Shades of solidarity: Comparing Scottish and Flemish responses to Catalonia. *Regional and Federal Studies*, 4 February (online).

Van Rompuy, Herman (2019). Herman Van Rompuy says Brexit 'has changed EU view of Scotland'. BBC. Available at www.bbc.co.uk/news/uk-scotla nd-scotland-politics-49690513 (accessed 25 August 2021).

Wolkenstein, Fabio (2018). Demoicracy, transnational partisanship and the EU. *JCMS: Journal of Common Market Studies*, 56 (2): 284–299.

122 *Appendix*

Appendix – List of interviews

The list of interviewees is ordered alphabetically. It provides the names of the interviewees, the status of the interviewees at the time of the interview, and the dates of the interviews. The interviewers are referred to here as NB (Niklas Bremberg) and RG (Richard Gillespie).

Note (a): interviews conducted prior to 2019 (for the research project 'The Dynamics of Nationalist Evolution in Contemporary Spain', ES/J007854/1) are referred to non-anonymized in the book chapters, whereas all interviews conducted in 2019–2021 (for the research project 'National independence and European integration: Scotland's and Catalonia's democratic challenges to the political order in the EU', MMW 2017.0027) are referred to anonymized (e.g. CAT 1 and SNP 1) so that opinions and views cannot be attributed to individual interviewees due to the fact that some issues discussed in relation to Scottish and Catalan independence claims were still considered politically sensitive at the time of writing. However, all the interviewees have agreed that their names may be included in the list below.

Note (b): due to travel restrictions imposed following the outbreak of the coronavirus (COVID-19) pandemic, all interviews conducted in 2020–2021 were held on Zoom.

Note (c): in the absence of a direct translation of the Catalan word *conseller*, referring to members of the Catalan Government, we use the latter's own translation of 'minister', while clarifying that this is in a regional context.

Interviewees

Amorós, Oriol, ERC, Catalan MP, 22 September 2014. RG.

Anglada, Marti, Secretary for Communication and Media Relations, Generalitat de Catalunya, 13 November 2019. NB.

Arrufat, Quim, CUP, Catalan MP, 12 February 2014. RG.

Borrell, Mireia, Secretary for Foreign Action and the EU, Generalitat de Catalunya, 14 November 2019. NB.

Bosch, Alfred, ERC, spokesperson for the ERC parliamentary group in the Congreso de los Diputados, 29 November 2013. RG.

Bosch, Alfred, ERC, regional Minister for Foreign Action, Institutional Relations and Transparency, Generalitat de Catalunya, 14 November 2019. NB.

Carod-Rovira, Josep-Lluís, former leader of ERC, 1996–2008, 13 February 2014. RG.

Corominas, Lluís, CDC, Catalan MP, 28 November 2013. RG.

Appendix 123

de Gispert, Núria, UDC, Catalan MP, speaker of the Catalan Parliament, 11 February 2014. RG.

Forcadell, Carme, President of the ANC, 26 November 2013. RG.

Gethins, Stephen, SNP spokesperson on Europe, 19 November 2020. NB.

Maragall, Ernest, Nova Esquerra Catalana (previously PSC, later ERC), 10 February 2014, RG.

McLeod, Aileen, SNP MEP, 6 November 2020. NB.

Puigdemont, Carles, CDC, Catalan MP, Mayor of Girona, 27 November 2013. RG.

Pujol, Jordi, former leader of CDC 1974–2003, former Catalan MP and President of the Generalitat, 1980–2003, 26 November 2013. RG.

Royo, Albert, former Diplocat Secretary-General, 14 November 2019. NB.

Vila, Santi, CDC, Catalan MP, regional Minister for Territory and Sustainability, Generalitat de Catalunya, 13 February 2014. RG.

Smith, Alyn, SNP MP for Stirling, 4 February 2021. NB.

Solé, Jordi, ERC, party Secretary for International Relations, 13 November 2019. NB.

Strubell, Toni, former Catalan MP for SI, 14 February 2014. RG.

Vilanova, Jordi, ERC, member of party Committee for International Relations, 13 November 2019. NB.

Index

Abts, K., Heerwegh, D. and Swyngedouw, M. 1
Adler-Nissen, Rebecca 5, 16
Akkerman, T., de Lange, S.L. and Rooduijn, M. 1
Alba ('Scotland' in Gaelic) Party 91; creation of, Salmond's announcement of 92
ABC 42
Amnesty International 63
Amorós, Oriol 29, 70, 109, 122
Anglada, Marti 122
Aragonès i Garcia, Pere 113
Arrufat, Quim 71, 122
Assemblea Nacional Catalana (ANC) 27, 58, 63, 70; formation of (May 2011) 53; massive demonstrations coordinated by, impact of EU of 72–3; secessionist turn in Catalan politics 55
Assembly of European Regions 38
Aumaitre, Ariane 68–9
Avui 43
Aznar, José María 33, 46

Balfour, S. and Quiroga, A. 31
Barberà, Ò. and Barrio, A. 38
Barcelona Declaration (1989) 40
Barrio, A. and Barberà, Ò 54
Barroso, José Manuel Durão 11, 56, 82
Bartolini, Stefano 7
Basque *fueros* 37
Bauböck, Rainer 7, 13

Bellamy, R. and Castiglione, D. 8
Bellamy, Richard 116
Bickerton, Christopher 8
Biermann, F. and Jagdhuber, S. 87
Borrell, Josep 94, 111
Borrell, Mireia 122
Bosch, Alfred 67, 70, 73, 109, 122
Bourgeois, Geert 110
Bremberg, N. and Norman, L. 116
Bremberg, Niklas 4, 8, 122–3
Brexit: Brexit referendum (2016) 1; Brexit referendum (2016), shock result for SNP 85; constitutional challenge for SNP in 83–7; constitutional crisis looming, Brexit and SNP stance on Scottish independence 91; doing Brexit but undoing UK? 88–90; 'Get Brexit done' slogan 89; leadership and public opinion on SNP post-Brexit 94–7; majority having voted against in Scotland 105; post-Brexit independence and integration in Europe for Scotland 90–93; Scotland, post-Brexit setting for independence claims 19; Scottish independence and integration in Europe post-Brexit 91, 92, 93; SNP constitutional challenge for UK and 83, 85, 86, 87; SNP gradualist discourse on national independence and 78; 'tricky issues' in post-Brexit setting for SNP 95–6

Index 125

British Broadcasting Corporation (BBC) 82, 83, 85–6, 91–2, 106, 111, 112; BBC Scotland 81
Buchanan, Allen E. 7
Bundesverfassungsgericht 7

Cameron, David 83, 85, 109
Caminal i Badia, Miquel 40
Canadian Clarity Act (1998) 7
Candidatura d'Unitat Popular (CUP) 31, 55, 103; critical stance towards EU 114; dissenting position on Europe 71; electoral results for 61, 62; independence for Catalonia, pursuit of 58; radical anti-capitalist grassroots movement 27; uncompromising programme (March 2021) 68; unilateralism, support for 112–13
Carod-Rovira, Josep-Lluís 31, 39, 40, 122
Catalan Parliament: referendum organization, opposition in 59; territorial preferences (2010–21) 54; vote to declare independence in (October 2017) 59–60
Catalan Socialist Party (PSC-PSOE) 62
Catalonia: agitation for referendum in 53; autonomy and independence for, traditional arguments for 28–30; bilateral consultations with Scottish government 109–11; Catalan autonomy, invocation of Article 155 of Spanish Constitution suspending (October 2017) 59–60; Catalan conflict, strategic efforts for 'internationalization' of 51–2; *catalanismo* in independence movement 29; combination of pro-independence and Eurosceptic attitudes in, prevalence of 97; Consell Assessor report on implications of independence for European membership 56; Constitution for Europe, debate on 40–44, 103–4; constitutional context and unsympathetic response of Rajoy Government in 104; contested meaning of

'Europe' in 113–17; cross-fertilization in EU between Scottish and Catalan pro-independence parties 107–13; cross-party united action in, need for 55–6; debates about 'Europe' in 46–7; devolution to, introduction of 37–8; Diplocat, creation of 55; early responses to European integration process in 32–3; elite views on Europe in 68–74; Europe, change in discourse among Catalan pro-independence forces on 64–8; Europe and, long-range perspective on 30–31; European integration, Catalan independence and 51–75; European integration process, early responses to 32–3; European issues, political divergence within 47; European Movement in, establishment of (1949) 33; Euroscepticism in, possibility of rise if EU opposition to self-determination persists 69–70; 'fiscal pact' with Spanish government, idea of (2010) 54; governmental assumptions on self-determination, basis for 72–3; grassroots demands for Catalan statehood 53–4; historical evolution of visions of 'Europe' in 27–8; historical status as engine room of industrialization in Spain 33; illegal referendum, attitude to parliamentary procedures and defiance of court injunctions in 108; independence challenge of, Spanish responses to 62–4; independence claims and risk of loss of EU membership 19; independence for, pursuit of 58–61; independence for, reasons underpinning claims for 18–19, 19–20; independence movement on EU and European integration, discourse of 52–4; independence of, EU competences and powers and 17; 'internationalize the Catalan conflict,' efforts towards

126 *Index*

51–2; 'more Catalonia' and 'more Europe' but not 'less Spain,' Mas' message of 57–8; nationalist parties in, participation in EU institutions by 108–9; parallels with Scotland 17–18; polarization in, referendum and 60–61; political dynamics surrounding regional secessionism and European integration in 3–5; positivity on Europe following 2017 events in 65–6, 73–4; pro-independence forces in, still betting on Brussels? 74–5; pro-independence movement in, evolution of 27–8; pro-independence politicians in, claims of 72; *procés* for independence in 27, 51, 63, 70, 71; *procés* for independence in, embryonic phase of 53; *procés* for independence in, imprisonment of leaders of 63; *procés* for independence in, launch of 58–61; public manifestations in support of independence for 2; public opinion on Europe in 68–74; Rajoy's policy on 56–7; rebuffs in Europe for independence leaders 105; regional autonomy in, re-establishment of 6; Scotland and, cases for independence compared 102–7; Scotland and, evolving and contrasting independence claims in 44–7; Scotland and, pro-independence parties in comparative perspective 28–31; secessionist turn in Catalan politics 55–8; semi-structured interviews with political representatives from 20; sovereignty, perspective on 45–6; 'Spain in Europe,' spearhead for 33; state investment in, poverty of 52; strategic divergence among pro-independence forces in 61–4; sympathy in Europe for pro-independence parties 106; Unilateral Declaration of Independence, initial

postponement by Puigdemont of 59; value to EU of, arguments for self-determination based on 71–2; Wert Law on language status 57; *see also* Generalitat de Catalunya
Centre d'Estudis d'Opinió (CEO) 4, 31
Cetrà, D. and Liñeira, R. 7, 70
Charter of Fundamental Rights 74
Checkel, J.T. and Katzenstein, P.J. 14
Cheneval, F. and Nicolaidis, K. 116
Cheneval, F. and Schimmelfennig, F. 116
Churchill, Winston 33
Ciudadanos (Cs) 60–61
Closa, Carlos 3
Colau, Ada 61
Colino, César 6
Comín, Antoni 62, 64
Committee of the Regions (CoR) 8, 9, 108, 118–19; independence in Europe, paths to 28, 37, 38, 41
Common Market 30; SNP perspective on 34
Common Travel Area (CTA) 81
Conservative Party in UK 79, 81, 82, 99, 114; Brexit and SNP's constitutional challenge for 83, 85, 86, 87; doing Brexit but undoing UK? 88, 89; Scottish independence and integration in Europe post-Brexit 91, 92, 93
Constitution for Europe: debate on 40–44, 103–4; 'European Constitution of the People and the Nations,' ERC preference for 43; European Convention on 41–2; rejection for proposal for 1; Scottish nationalist objections to draft treaty 41; Spanish referendum on (2005) 43
Convergència Democràtica de Catalunya (CDC) 54, 58, 60, 68, 70, 109; Catalonia as pro-European link for Spain, Pujol's perspective on 33; Constitution of Europe, debate on 42, 43–4, 46; creation of (1974) 30; 'free and sovereign nation in 21st century Europe, vote for (July

2008) 53; integration of Spain in European institutions, support for 38; outreach to other pro-sovereignty groups 55; party behaviour, structural influences informing 42; sovereignty and independence, shift in emphasis towards 47; 'state of our own,' adoption of objective of 27, 31; unity of CiU in support for 'yes' vote in Spanish referendum (2005) 43
Convergència i Unió (CiU) 27, 29, 34, 37, 40, 53, 62, 103; breakup of, post-CDC division and 68; Catalan as an official language of EU, desire for 64–5; Catalan nationalism, early history of CiU and 33; Europhilia of, unreserved 103; operations at EU level through regional government activities, success in 45–6; paradiplomacy in Europe, opportunities for 108; pragmatic collaboration with Spanish government, and lack of criticism of EC from 38; pro-European mindset of 41–2; programme for 2010 Catalan elections 54; repeated success in regional elections 45; secessionist turn in Catalan politics 55; support for process of European integration from 38–9; eventual unity in support for 'yes' vote in Spanish referendum (2005) 43
Corominas, Lluís 70, 122
Council of Europe, Parliamentary Assembly of 63
Court of Justice of the EU (CJEU) 12–13, 62, 74, 82
COVID-19 pandemic 61, 74, 90–91, 92–3, 122
Cram, Laura 10, 113
Crameri, Kathryn 38, 53
Crimea case as warning against secessionism 109
Cuadras-Morató, Xavier 3
Culla i Clarà, Juan B. 33, 39
Curtice, J. and Montagu, I. 14; Scottish independence in

integrated Europe, viability of 94, 96, 97
Curtice, John 88

Dalle Mulle, E. and Serrano, I. 3
Darling, Alistair 81
Davidson, Ruth 82, 84
Davis, David 87
De Gispert, Núria 33, 70, 123
De la Fuente, Ángel 72
De Vries, Catherine E. 1
Decidem! 52
Delors, Jacques 35
democracy 70, 74, 84, 102, 109; citizenship and 8; community among peoples and 119; diversity and, promotion of 67; Europe as emblem of freedom and 30; human rights, freedom and 18, 80; independence claims and notions of 115; liberal democracy, transition of Spain to 37; notion of, deep connections to independence 115–16; participatory democracy, cohesion and 67; protection of, Scottish independence and 94, 99; quality in host states of, concerns about 118; Scotland, relationship with democracy in Britain 29; Scottish National Party (SNP) and question of 89–90; social democracy, Scandinavian-style 98; sovereignty and 1; in Spain, Europe as safeguard for 30–31
Democratic Unionist Party (DUP) in Northern Ireland 86, 87
Diada 53, 55, 57
Diamond, P., Nedergaard, P. and Rosamond, B. 87
El Diario.es 60
Diez Medrano, Juan 14
Dion, Stéphane 7
discourse analysis 20
Dowling, Andrew 30, 32, 42, 53, 54
Duerr, Glen M.E. 5, 71, 109

The Economist 55
Edward, Sir David 82

128 *Index*

Elias, Anwen 4, 9, 42
Elliot, John 7, 19, 29, 102, 118
Esquerra Republicana de Catalunya (ERC) 17, 19, 27, 30, 45, 46, 60–61, 62, 70; Catalonia and Scotland, comparisons and implications 103, 107, 109, 112–13; 'Catalonia's major left-wing national party' 29; Consell Català del Moviment Europeu, involvement with 33; consensus between ERC and JxCat on European issues 64–5; Constitutional Treaty, call for 'no' vote on draft of 43; demonstration in Brussels by Catalan pro-independence civil society groups, backing for 53; differences between ERC and JxCat on European issues, growth of 67, 75; independence, adoption as official objective (1989) 31; intense interparty competition between CiU and 42; Junts pel Sí (JxSí), presentation of common list in 58; political resolution, passing of (November 2019) 65–6; positioning distinct yet similar to that of CiU 39–40; pro-independence programme, campaign on (2010) 54; repression under Franco regime 32; secessionist turn in Catalan politics and 55; sovereignty and independence politics, shift towards (2017) 47
Estonia, support for Catalan referendum from 71
Eurobarometer 1
'Europe': belonging to, notion of 114–15; Catalan pro-independence parties, contested meaning for 113–14; Scottish independence claims and evolution of SNP discourse on 114
'Europe of the Regions' idea, Pujol's support for 38
European Commission 8, 56, 70, 71, 74, 82; Catalonia and Scotland, comparisons and implications 104,

105, 119; Future of Europe, white paper on (2017) 67; interpretation of EU treaties based on non-existent exclusion mechanism 12; response to regional succession in EU 11–14; social Europe, presentation by 35
European Community (EC)/ European Union (EU) 28, 38, 41–2, 44, 45, 46, 47, 103
European Council 8, 71, 88, 99, 106
European Economic Community (EEC) 30, 32, 33
European Free Alliance (EFA) 65–6, 108–9
European Free Trade Association (EFTA) 92
European Parliament 9, 36, 37, 43, 60, 62, 71, 105; powers of, periodic enhancements of 45–6; SNP manifesto for 2014 elections to 81
European Union (EU) 51; attachment of people to 'Europe' 16; Catalonia, trust in by territorial preference for 69; collective identities, determination of dynamics of 15; collective identities, reinforcement of 14; Common Fisheries Policy 45; consolidation of, incorporation of Spain and 38; 'constraining dissensus' in politics of 1; constructivist understanding of political communities in 15–16; coordination problems following enlargement 104; 'core state functions,' integration into political system of 8; 'democratic deficit' in EU decision-making 8–9; democratic foundations of political order in 14–19; enlargement 36; EU-Catalonia Platform for Dialogue 74; European integration, attractiveness of independence and 4–5; failed democracy in, charges of 64; independence claims, mobilizing potential of 5; institutional developments 34–5,

37, 40; integration in, territorial tensions and 8; Mediterranean policy 45; national identities, dynamics surrounding 5; national identities, relationship between European integration and 15; non-sovereign regions in, popular support for independence of 2; normative foundations of political order in 14–19; 'permissive consensus' in politics of 1; policymaking process in, control of 1; political dynamics surrounding regional secessionism and European integration in 3–5; popular support for membership 1–2; post-functionalist theory of European integration 14–15; 'post-sovereign' political system of 8; pro-independence political parties, electoral successes of 9; Prodi doctrine 11–14, 21n1, 82; region level political institutions, strengthening of 9; regional secessionism and integration in, competing views on 9–11; regional secessionism and integration in, historical perspective on 5–9; regional secessionism in 3, 7–8, 8–9; regional secessionism in, democratic challenge to political order 117–19; risk-taking among citizens, uncertainty and 13–14; secessionist movements in member states 2; sovereignty and democracy, politicization and contestation about 1; state-building in Europe, classic works on 5–6; stateless nations in, popular support for independence of 2; structural funding, changes in (1980s and 1990s) 9; 'territorial rescaling' 13; theoretical expectations, previous research and 4–5, 10, 14; treaty changes 34–40; unitary and federal states, differences between 6–7; viability theory 10–11
Europeanization strategies, effectiveness of 105

Eurosceptic perspectives 1, 2, 42, 44, 53, 73, 75, 83; Catalan Euroscepticism, neutralization of temptations towards 65–6; Catalan Euroscepticism, potential justification for 70; Scotland, Eurosceptic attitudes in 32, 34–5, 41, 96–7
Euskadi 37, 44
Euskadi ta Azkatasuna (Basque Homeland and Liberty) 51

Farage, Nigel 83, 88
Favell, Adrian 14
Field, Bonnie C. 43
Figueira, F. and Martill, B. 87
Financial Times 52
Fligstein, Neil 14
Føllesdal, A. and Hix, S. 8
Forcadell, Carme 70, 123
Franco, Francisco 32–3, 34
Francoist era (1939–1976) 30, 37

Gardner, David 52, 109
Generalitat de Catalunya 6, 30, 103, 107, 112–13; European integration, Catalan independence and 54, 56, 57, 58, 67, 73; *Pla Europa* white paper by JxCat-ERC coalition (2018–2020) 67
Genschel, P. and Jachtenfuchs, M. 8
German Constitutional Court ruling (2016) on Bavarian referendum 7, 10
Gethins, Stephen 123
Gillespie, Richard 31, 42, 44, 51, 122–3
González, Felipe 37–8
Gove, Michael 83
Gray, Caroline 37, 52, 54
Green Party in UK 83
The Guardian 85, 111, 112
Guibernau, Montserrat 38, 40

Haas, Ernst 21n2
Hanvey, Neale 92
Harteveld, E., van der Meer, T. and Vries, C.E. 14
Hepburn, Eve 4, 9, 30, 37, 41
Hix, Simon 87

130 *Index*

Hobolt, S.B. and Tilley, J. 1
Hollande, François 85
Hooghe, L. and Marks, G. 1, 5, 14, 15, 115
Howarth, Jolyon 104
Human Rights, European Convention on 87

Illa, Salvador 62
The Independent 112
Iniciativa per Catalunya Verds (ICV) 43, 65–6, 109
Institut de Ciències Polítiques i Socials (ICPS) 31
Ipsos MORI 31

Jackson, Ben 30, 99–100n1
Jenkins, Blair 81
Johnson, Boris 83, 87, 88, 89, 99, 113
Jolly, Seth K. 4, 10, 113; independence in Europe, paths to 30, 34–5, 36, 37, 41–2
Jordana, J., Keating, M., Marx, A. and Wouters, J. 7
Juncker, Jean-Claude 11, 110; Catalan independence, European integration and 64, 73; Scottish independence in integrated Europe, viability of 82, 85
Junqueras, Oriol 17, 31, 109, 113; Catalan independence, European integration and 55, 62, 74
Junts pel Sí (JxSí) 58, 65
Junts per Catalunya (JxCat) 68, 75, 112, 113; Catalan independence, pursuit of 60–61; divergent strategies among Catalan pro-independence forces 62; Europe, changing discourses among Catalan pro-independence forces on 64, 65, 66–7

Keating, M. and McEwan, N. 80
Keating, M., Jordana, J., Marx, A. and Wouters, J. 5, 16, 116
Keating, Michael 6, 7, 8, 29, 82, 118, 119
Kenealy, Daniel 9, 12–13, 82
Kornprobst, Markus 7

Kriesi, Hanspeter 1
Kurdish secessionists, Turkish treatment of 63

Labour Party in Scotland 32, 34–5, 79, 84
Labour Party in UK 81–2, 83, 86, 88, 91
Laible, Janet 4, 10, 108, 113; independence in Europe, paths to 29, 32, 34, 35, 36
Liberal Democrats in UK 79, 81, 83, 85, 88, 91
Liñeira, R. and Cetrà, D. 3
Linz, J.J. and Stepan, A. 8
Lithuania, support for Catalan referendum from 71
Longoria, Álvaro 64
Lynch, Peter 32, 34–5, 36, 108–9

MacAskill, Kenny 92
MacCormick, Neil 12
McLeod, Aileen 123
McNamara, Kathleen R. 5, 16
McTavish, D. and Garnett, M. 6, 79
Madrid Parliament 38, 45, 54
Mair, Peter 8
Majone, Giandomenico 8
Manners, Ian 5, 16
Maragall, Ernest 70, 123
Maragall, Pasqual 42
Marcet, J. and Argelaguet, J. 38, 39
Marks, G., Hooghe, L. and Blank, K. 9
Mas, Artur 27, 42; Catalan independence, European integration and 53, 55–6, 57–8
May, Theresa 83, 85, 87, 88
Members of the European Parliament (MEPs) 62–3, 74
Minder, Raphael 108
Moravcsik, Andrew 8, 21n2
Moreno, Luis 6
Müller, Jan-Werner 1
El Mundo 71
Muro, D. and Vlaskamp, M. 14, 69, 96–7

Nagel, Klaus-Jürgen 30, 38, 41, 53
National Health Service (NHS) 92

Index 131

nationhood, competing visions of 6
Navarra 37, 44
Newell, James L. 30, 36
Nieuw-Vlaamse Alliantie 110
Norman, Ludvig 1
North Atlantic Treaty Organization
(NATO) 81, 94

Olivares, Gerardo 64
Òmnium Cultural 27, 52, 59, 63
Organisation for Economic
Co-operation and Development
(OECD) 33
Ortega y Gasset, José 107

El País 42; Catalan independence,
European integration and 53, 57,
63, 64, 71, 72, 74; Scotland and
Catalonia, comparisons and
implications 107, 109, 111, 113
Partido Popular (PP) 38; Catalan
independence, European
integration and 54, 56, 61
Partido Popular-Vox coalition 107
Partido Socialista Obrero Español
(PSOE) 38, 39, 63, 94, 111
Partit dels Socialistes de Catalunya
(PSC) 39, 57, 70, 75
Partit Demòcrata Europeu Català
(PDeCAT) 60, 62, 68
El Periódico de Catalunya 60, 74,
110
Piris, Jean-Claude 11
Plaid Cymru in Wales 83
Plataforma pel Dret de Decidir 52
Politico 111
Ponsatí, Clara 62, 111–12
Powell, Charles 30
Prat, Juan 55–6
Prodi, Romano 11; Prodi doctrine
11–14, 21n1, 82
PSOE-Unidas Podemos (UP)
coalition 61
Puigdemont, Carles 17, 96, 123;
Catalan independence, European
integration and 58, 59, 60, 61, 62,
64, 74; Scotland and Catalonia,
comparisons and implications 107,
110, 112, 114
Pujol, Jordi 29, 33, 38, 41, 60, 123

Rajoy, Mariano (and government of)
85; Catalan independence,
European integration and 55, 56,
59, 63, 64, 73; Scotland and
Catalonia, comparisons and
implications 104, 106, 109,
111
Reding, Viviane 71
Reinikainen, Jouni 7
research design 19–20
Roeder, Philip G. 7
Rokkan, S. and Urwin, D.W. 6
Romeva, Raül 58
Royo, Albert 123
Rydgren, Jens 1

Salmond, Alex 35, 109, 110; High
Court acquittal in case against 91;
Scottish independence in
integrated Europe 80, 81, 82,
91–2, 96, 99–100n1
Sánchez, Pedro (and government of)
61, 63, 74; Scotland and
Catalonia, comparisons and
implications 104, 106–7, 111, 112
Schulz, Martin 85, 110
ScotCen Social Research 4
Scothorne, Rory 92
Scotland: 'Better Together' campaign
81–2; bilateral consultations with
Catalan government 109–11;
Catalonia and, cases for
independence compared 102–7;
Catalonia and, evolving and
contrasting independence claims
in 44–7; Catalonia and,
pro-independence parties in
comparative perspective 28–31;
choice between two unions for?
98–9; combination of
pro-independence and Eurosceptic
attitudes in, prevalence of 97;
contested meaning of 'Europe' in
113–17; COVID-19 pandemic in
91, 92–3; cross-fertilization in EU
between Catalan and Scottish
pro-independence parties 107–13;
'devolved competencies,' transfer
to Scottish Parliament 6–7; early
responses to European integration

132 *Index*

process in 32–3; elections in (2007–2021), results of 79; elections in (May 2016) 84; 'Europe,' divisiveness of issue in politics of 99; Europe and, long-range perspective on 30–31; European integration process, early responses to 32; European issues, political divergence within 47; Eurosceptic attitudes, relative persistence in 96; historical evolution of visions of 'Europe' in 27–8; independence debate, UK secession from EU and transformation of 105–6; independence for, reasons underpinning claims for 18–19, 19–20; loss of EU membership, effect on opinion of risk of 96–7; majority having voted against Brexit in 105; North Sea oil and future of 36; parallels with Catalonia 17–18; Parliamentary elections in (2021) 91; political dynamics surrounding regional secessionism and European integration in 3–5; post-Brexit independence and integration in Europe for 90–93; post-Brexit setting for independence claims 19; pro-independence movement in, evolution of 27–8; public attitudes (2013–2021) towards EU in 97; public manifestations in support of independence for 2; Scotland Act (1998, UK Parliament) 6–7, 31; *Scotland Analysis* (UK government paper) 81–2; Scottish independence and EU membership, uncertainties surrounding 82; Scottish independence in integrated Europe 78–100; semi-structured interviews with political representatives from 20; sovereignty, SNP perspective on 45; United Kingdom (UK) and, Brexit and potential for undoing UK? 88–90; 'Yes Scotland' campaign 81
Scottish Conservatives 35, 84

Scottish Government 80–81, 85, 87, 93
Scottish Green Party 91–2
Scottish National Party (SNP) 18, 19, 27; agreement with UK for second independence referendum, pressure on 96; Brexit and constitutional challenge for 83–7; Brexit referendum (2016), shock result for 85; Catalan case for independence, reality of different circumstances in Scotland for 108; Catalan conflict, positions of leadership on 111; Catalonia and Scotland, comparisons and implications 103, 104, 105–6, 108, 110–11, 112–13, 114–15; choice between two unions for? 98–9; Common Market, perspective on 34; constitutional crisis looming, Brexit and SNP stance on Scottish independence 91; constitutional debate, tone during 41; democracy, question for 89–90; democracy, question of 89–90; 'democratic mandate' for second independence referendum 86, 89–90; discourse on 'Europe,' changes in 46; electoral manifesto, UK general election (2017) 86; electoral manifesto, UK general election (2019) 89–90; electoral manifesto (2011) 79; electoral manifesto (2016) 84; 'Europe,' Scottish independence claims and evolution of discourse on 114; European Community (EC), shift towards positivity on (1980s) 35–6; European integration process, early responses to 32; European Parliament, manifesto for 2014 elections to 81; Euroscepticism of (1960s) 34; governing party, consolidation of position as 78; independence and European integration, visions in 2021 manifesto 93; independence claims in Scotland and Catalonia, evolution of and contrasts in 44, 45, 46–7; 'Independence in

Index 133

Europe,' adoption of slogan by 36–7; 'instrumental in their support' for EU 103; leadership and public opinion post-Brexit 94–7; leadership of, Salmond's criticisms of 92; legal basis for referendum, negotiation of 80; membership of EU and NATO, 'cornerstones of independence for 94–5; 'natural position' as active participant in EU 80; participation in EU institutions by 108–9; political campaigns that preceded 2014 referendum 81–2; positions on Europe, electoral considerations and 34–5; post-Brexit independence and integration in Europe for 90–93; pro-independence parties in Catalonia and Scotland, comparative perspective on 28–9, 30, 31; referendum on independence, promise of (2011) 80; relations with Generalitat in Catalonia, caution on 112; representation by UK government, criticisms of 105; *Scotland's Future* (SNP government white paper) 80–81; Scotland's place in 'Europe,' vision for 87; *Scotland's Place in Europe* (SNP government report) 85; Scottish election (2011), results for 80–81; Scottish referendum (2014) and discourse on Europe 78–83; socio-economic and sectoral interests, Euroscepticism on 32; sovereignty of Scotland, perspective on 45; Sturgeon elected leader of (2014) 82–3; treaty changes, institutional developments and EU enlargement 34–7; 'tricky issues' in post-Brexit setting for 95–6; UK general election (2015), landslide victory for 83; vision of independence, longstanding nature of 78–9
secession (and secessionism): citizenship and democracy in

Europe and 8; Crimea case as warning against 109; rarity of phenomenon 7; regional secessionism 3, 4, 14, 16, 20–21, 47, 116; regional secessionism, competing views on European integration and 9–11; regional secessionism, democratic challenge to EU political order and 117–19; regional secessionism, European Commission response to 11–14; regional secessionism, European integration in historical perspective and 5–9; secessionist movements in EU member states 2; sovereignty claims and 3, 9
Seubert, S., Eberl, O. and van Waarden, F. 8
Siddiqui, Mona 83
Sijstermans, J. and Brown Swan, C. 108, 110
Sillars, Jim 83, 99–100n1
Single European Act 28
Smith, Alyn 123
Smith, Ángel 33
Smith of Kelvin, Lord Robert (and Smith Commission) 83, 95
Sobirania i Justícia 52
Sobirania i Progrés 52
Solé, Jordi 123
Solidaritat Catalana per la Independència (SI) 55, 71
Sorens, Jason 7
Soviet Union: demise of 7; independence of the Baltic countries from 40
Spain: Catalan independence challenge, responses to 62–4; Catalonia and, dialogue between (2021) 106–7; *comunidades autónomas* in 31; Congress of Deputies in 38, 43–4, 45; Constitution for Europe, referendum on (2005) 43; Constitutional Court of 10, 17, 52, 53, 55, 57, 58, 103; debates about 'Europe' in 46–7; democracy in, Europe as safeguard for 30–31; invocation of Article 155 of Constitution suspending Catalan

134   *Index*

autonomy (October 2017) 59–60; 'judicialization' of policy on Catalonia 111–12; liberal democracy, transition to 37; Ministry of Foreign Affairs 71; Spanish External Action Law 56–7; territorial integrity of 17
Strubell, Miquel 52, 71, 108
Strubell, Toni 123
Sturgeon, Nicola 18, 60; condemnation of long sentences against Catalan leaders 111; 'double majority' requirement for UK withdrawal from EU (2015) 84–5; 'entirely legitimate' for Spain to oppose independence for Catalonia (2017) 110; ministerial code breach by, independent inquiry on 91; Scotland and Catalonia, comparisons and implications 110–11, 112; Scottish independence in integrated Europe 82–3, 84, 85, 89, 90, 92; UK withdrawal from EU, statement following 90

Tajani, Antonio 62, 64
Thatcher, Margaret 31
Thompson, Helen 92
Tilly, Charles 6
The Times 94
Timmermans, Frans 74
Torra i Pla, Quim 61, 67, 110, 112
Torreblanca, José I. 43
Treaty of Rome (1957) 32
Treaty on European Union (TEU) 8, 9, 11–12, 18; independence in Europe, paths to 28, 39, 46–7; Scottish independence in integrated Europe 82, 85, 86
Treaty on the Functioning of the European Union (TFEU) 12
Two Catalonias (documentary) 64

UNESCO, Club d'Amics de la 33
Unidas Podemos (UP) 61, 63
Unió Democràtica de Catalunya (UDC) 27, 30, 38, 70; European Convention, 'positive' aspects in

draft for 42, 43; European Free Alliance (EFA) and 109
United Kingdom (UK): agreement reached by May government with EU, criticisms of 87; Brexit referendum in (2016) 1; 'Britain Stronger in Europe' campaign 83; constitutional crisis looming, Brexit and SNP stance on Scottish independence 91; enactment of Article 50 of TEU 17–18, 85–6; general election (2017) 86; general election (2019), Johnson government and 89; 'Get Brexit done' slogan 89; government 78, 80, 83, 84, 88, 89, 93, 95, 96, 99; independence debate, UK secession from EU and transformation of 105–6; *Scotland Analysis* paper (January 2014) 81–2; Scottish Affairs Committee of House of Commons 82; terms of withdrawal from EU, initiation of negotiations (2017) 87; transition period following EU-UK withdrawal agreement 90–91; 'Vote Leave' campaign 83; withdrawal negotiations with EU, start of (2016) 85–6
United Nations, creation of 6
Universitat Oberta de Catalunya, poll by (2010) 53

Van Middelaar, Luuk 8
Van Rompuy, Herman 106
La Vanguardia 43, 57
Verhofstadt, Guy 85
Vila, Santi 70, 123
Vilanova, Jordi 123
Vlaams Belang 2

Weiler, Joseph H.H. 12
Wilson, Gordon 36
Wolkenstein, Fabio 116

Yugoslavia, break-up of 7, 40

Zapatero, José Luis Rodríguez 42–3, 46

Ingram Content Group UK Ltd.
Milton Keynes UK
UKHW052242100523
421267UK00030B/120